AF772088

CHALLENGES AND OPPORTUNITIES FOR U.S. POLICY IN THE WESTERN HEMISPHERE

TUESDAY, OCTOBER 21, 2003

HOUSE OF REPRESENTATIVES,
SUBCOMMITTEE ON THE WESTERN HEMISPHERE,
COMMITTEE ON INTERNATIONAL RELATIONS,
Washington, DC.

The Subcommittee met, pursuant to call, at 2:10 p.m. in Room 2200, Rayburn House Office Building, Hon. Cass Ballenger (Chairman of the Subcommittee) presiding.

Mr. BALLENGER. The Subcommittee will come to order. This afternoon we explore challenges and opportunities for United States policy in the Western Hemisphere.

It is a pleasure to welcome our first panel of witnesses from the Bush Administration, including at long last Senate-confirmed Assistant Secretary of State for the Western Hemisphere. We are also pleased to have a second panel that will feature Dr. Robert Pastor, a former senior policymaker, and scholar of United States relations with the Americas.

Assistant Secretary Roger Noriega and USAID Assistant Administrator, Adolfo Franco, are well known to me and to Members of the International Relations Committee, and need little introduction.

In my considered opinion, President Bush has signaled his commitment to the Western Hemisphere by appointing these two very capable gentlemen.

Events just this past week in Bolivia remind us that there are nations in the Western Hemisphere that face grave challenges, and we are all appalled by the violence in Bolivia, but we all urge Bolivians to reject violence and respect democratic institutions and constitutional order.

The euphoria of the nineties has dissipated in the Western Hemisphere. Incomplete economic reforms have collided with the worldwide recession and implosion in some countries of traditional political parties. The truth is that some governments in this hemisphere have not been able to extend education and economic opportunities to poor communities, while endemic corruption saps money from the real priorities. In some countries there are political parties and political movements led by demagogues that use violence as a political tool, and even shield criminals and terrorists.

There is good news too. Democracy is firm in English-speaking Caribbean. President Uribe with our help is giving Colombia's democracy a real chance to survive and prosper. Soon the Colombian people will again vote in municipal elections despite threats and attacks by terrorist groups like the FARC.

Brazil is a stable democracy that can exercise positive influence in South America, and Mexico's President Vincente Fox has made real progress in going after major drug traffickers and criminals. Chile has demonstrated that sustained economic reform and adherence to democracy benefits ordinary people. El Salvador continues to demonstrate that sustained engagement by U.S., coupled with political will from the country's leaders, creates real reforms.

Now it is time for the leaders in this hemisphere who believe in democracy and liberating power of the private power sector economics to stand up and work together. We must not let the lesser matters divide us. I believe it is time that Congress and the Administration rethink the focus and scope of our foreign assistance programs in this hemisphere.

It is not just that we are providing the kind of money we should, we must also engage our friends and neighbors with a new entrepreneurial approaches to create wealth for the people and for our own people, and I know that our witnesses understand the challenge of our nation and our friends and our neighbors in this hemisphere face.

I also believe that our testimony today can help identify the opportunities that will allow us all to move forward in positive, ways, and I would like to recognize the Ranking Member, the ranking Democratic, my friend, Mr. Menendez, for an opening statement.

Mr. MENENDEZ. Thank you, Mr. Chairman, and let me—there has been very little disagreement between us, and I want to join with you in saying that if the measure of the Administration's commitment to Latin America is based on the distinguished gentlemen before us, then it is a huge commitment, and we appreciate that.

But there are other measurements that I would like to talk about, and I do not dispute that these two fine gentlemen are tremendous assets to the United States in promoting our interests in the hemisphere. I thank them for coming today as well as Dr. Pastor.

And I want to thank you, Mr. Chairman, for holding this hearing. We are here today to finally focus our attention on Latin America, and I believe it is time that we did, and I hope that as a Committee we do more to highlight the serious problems the region is facing and to seek solutions.

We have held very few hearings this session, and I hope that we will do much more. It is certainly not enough for a region which some refer to as our back yard, but I would like to say as our front yard, our neighbors, and our partners. It is not enough for a region which has been all but abandoned by this Administration.

This Administration's Latin America policy is more notable for the lack of a policy than for any specific or coherent policy, and the Administration's myopic tendency to rush in when there is a problem, and ignore the region the rest of the time only undermines our credibility in Latin America.

As we end the 3rd year of this Administration, what real policy achievements do we have to show? I would argue very little. This Administration has focused all of their attention on promoting free trade and ending the drug trade, but free trade alone will not ad-

CHALLENGES AND OPPORTUNITIES FOR U.S. POLICY IN THE WESTERN HEMISPHERE

HEARING

BEFORE THE

SUBCOMMITTEE ON
THE WESTERN HEMISPHERE

OF THE

COMMITTEE ON
INTERNATIONAL RELATIONS
HOUSE OF REPRESENTATIVES

ONE HUNDRED EIGHTH CONGRESS

FIRST SESSION

OCTOBER 21, 2003

Serial No. 108–65

Printed for the use of the Committee on International Relations

Available via the World Wide Web: http://www.house.gov/international_relations

U.S. GOVERNMENT PRINTING OFFICE

90–359PDF WASHINGTON : 2004

For sale by the Superintendent of Documents, U.S. Government Printing Office
Internet: bookstore.gpo.gov Phone: toll free (866) 512–1800; DC area (202) 512–1800
Fax: (202) 512–2250 Mail: Stop SSOP, Washington, DC 20402–0001

COMMITTEE ON INTERNATIONAL RELATIONS

HENRY J. HYDE, Illinois, *Chairman*

JAMES A. LEACH, Iowa
DOUG BEREUTER, Nebraska
CHRISTOPHER H. SMITH, New Jersey, *Vice Chairman*
DAN BURTON, Indiana
ELTON GALLEGLY, California
ILEANA ROS-LEHTINEN, Florida
CASS BALLENGER, North Carolina
DANA ROHRABACHER, California
EDWARD R. ROYCE, California
PETER T. KING, New York
STEVE CHABOT, Ohio
AMO HOUGHTON, New York
JOHN M. MCHUGH, New York
THOMAS G. TANCREDO, Colorado
RON PAUL, Texas
NICK SMITH, Michigan
JOSEPH R. PITTS, Pennsylvania
JEFF FLAKE, Arizona
JO ANN DAVIS, Virginia
MARK GREEN, Wisconsin
JERRY WELLER, Illinois
MIKE PENCE, Indiana
THADDEUS G. MCCOTTER, Michigan
WILLIAM J. JANKLOW, South Dakota
KATHERINE HARRIS, Florida

TOM LANTOS, California
HOWARD L. BERMAN, California
GARY L. ACKERMAN, New York
ENI F.H. FALEOMAVAEGA, American Samoa
DONALD M. PAYNE, New Jersey
ROBERT MENENDEZ, New Jersey
SHERROD BROWN, Ohio
CYNTHIA A. MCKINNEY, Georgia
EARL F. HILLIARD, Alabama
BRAD SHERMAN, California
ROBERT WEXLER, Florida
JIM DAVIS, Florida
ELIOT L. ENGEL, New York
WILLIAM D. DELAHUNT, Massachusetts
GREGORY W. MEEKS, New York
BARBARA LEE, California
JOSEPH CROWLEY, New York
JOSEPH M. HOEFFEL, Pennsylvania
EARL BLUMENAUER, Oregon
SHELLEY BERKLEY, Nevada
GRACE F. NAPOLITANO, California
ADAM B. SCHIFF, California
DIANE E. WATSON, California

THOMAS E. MOONEY, SR., *Staff Director/General Counsel*
ROBERT R. KING, *Democratic Staff Director*

SUBCOMMITTEE ON THE WESTERN HEMISPHERE

CASS BALLENGER, North Carolina, *Chairman*

RON PAUL, Texas
JERRY WELLER, Illinois
KATHERINE HARRIS, Florida
JAMES A. LEACH, Iowa
ILEANA ROS-LEHTINEN, Florida

ROBERT MENENDEZ, New Jersey
WILLIAM D. DELAHUNT, Massachusetts
GRACE NAPOLITANO, California
ENI F.H. FALEOMAVAEGA, American Samoa
DONALD M. PAYNE, New Jersey

CALEB MCCARRY, *Subcommittee Staff Director*
JESSICA LEWIS, *Democratic Professional Staff Member*
TED BRENNAN, *Professional Staff Member*
JEAN CARROLL, *Staff Associate*

CONTENTS

Page

WITNESSES

LETTERS, STATEMENTS, ETC., SUBMITTED FOR THE HEARING

APPENDIX

dress the real problems that threaten democracy and development in the region.

The President of the Intra-American Development Bank, Enrique Iglesias, was in my office a few months ago, and he said something very interesting for those who think that free trade alone will improve the developing world. He said we have so far lost the debate, and he was referring to within the hemisphere, and I believe we have. The people of Latin America and the Caribbean do not believe in the economic reforms of the 1990s, or that democracy necessarily brings good things to life. We know differently, but that is a prevailing view.

Take a look at the turmoil in Bolivia, Venezuela, just to name a few, and you come to understand the widespread disaffection in citizens throughout the hemisphere toward what is called the Washington consensus.

And so the region, in my view, is at a precarious moment. Yes, we have achieved democracy in the hemisphere with the notable exception of Cuba. Yet many of those democracies teeter at the edge. Recent events in Bolivia over the past few days highlight the fragility of that democracy. I am happy to see that Bolivia resolved this crisis without additional violence, and I encourage all to continue with a democratic transition to a new government.

But the people of Bolivia must understand that solving Bolivia's significant problems will take more than the 90 days the protesters have recently set aside for a truce, and I urge Mr. Morales, who believes that 90 days is all that is necessary, and that I think sets the basis on which a new protest takes place, and the possibility of democratic constitutional government is undermined, to work constructively for a peaceful solution.

And I also think that there are other things that this Administration can do with reference to Mr. Morales, and I will defer to Mr. Delahunt on some of those views.

Now, we, in the United States, have to take a good, hard look at the reality in Latin America that contributes to this instability. Almost a third of the region's population lives in poverty, and extreme poverty is growing. Fifty-nine million people live on less than a dollar a day. Eleven million more people suffer from extreme poverty today than in 1990. The region's children bear the brunt of poverty. Almost half of the region's children, 44 percent, live in an impoverished home. Almost 55 million people in Latin America and the Caribbean still suffer from hunger or malnutrition, and this is why we must have a clear vision for United States policy in Latin America.

We must show the people of Latin America that the United States is committed to their development, and to democracy, and that is why I will be asking Congress to create the Social Investment Fund for Latin America. And I know my good friend, Mr. Delahunt, will be introducing a bill to create a new permanent institute for democracy in the Western Hemisphere.

A new social investment from the Americas will invest money in things that affect the daily lives of Latin Americans, will invest in education, and health care, and economic development throughout the region.

Well, this fund will also benefit us here in the United States. It will create more demand for U.S. goods in a region of 500 million people. It will create greater economic growth so that the people will not have to leave their homes and their countries to find job. It will lift people out of poverty and create more political stability. It will reduce illegal immigration. With greater political stability and better economic growth, this fund will help be part of curing two of the main causes of illegal immigration.

These two initiatives are our first step toward creating a more coherent policy that addresses the urgent needs of Latin America, and I look forward to working with my colleagues on both side of the aisle, and I appreciate, Mr. Chairman, your commitment to having hearings on the Social Investment Fund, and Mr. Delahunt's legislation as well, as we move forward with these initiatives.

And finally, I would like to take a few minutes to highlight some specific areas of concern in the region. Let me start by discussing the new Central American Free Trade Agreement.

This Administration has heralded CAFTA not only for its impact on free trade, but also as the new plan which will lift Central America out of poverty, create democracy, and stability in the region. I hope we are careful not to exaggerate the impact of free trade. Let us be honest. Free trade does not address the deep-rooted problems of poverty and inequality in Central America.

The CAFTA agreement, I believe, must enforce strong labor and environmental standards. It is not enough that the new labor laws meet international standards, countries must show that they will enforce those laws on the ground.

And in addition, countries must show a commitment to the rule of law so that investors can count on a stable environment. And I am deeply concerned in particular about two of the proposed CAFTA countries.

Let me start with the Dominican Republic. After the fastest economic growth in Latin America at the end of the nineties, the Dominican Republic recently faced a serious economic crisis when Banco Intercontinental failed due to massive banking fraud. The government bailed them out for a price of $2.2 billion, and then took over the newspaper, radio, and television stations owned by the bank, prompting additional criticism that the government would use this to silence the opposition.

There are also allegations that the Dominican government was using a credit card issued by Banco Intercontinental on which millions of dollars were charged, but never repaid. And there are additional allegations that the Dominicans purchasing high-tech spy technology equipment from Israel for its own security subsequently had that equipment sold to the Castro regime.

Is this the kind of environment we want for United States companies who will invest in the Dominican Republic?

And Guatemala is fast becoming a narco state. Right now drugs flow into the United States from Colombia go through, around or over Guatemala. We see a devastating impact on both countries. In a strong move at the beginning of the year, the Administration decertified Guatemala, and since that time Guatemala has made some improvements in stopping the flow of drugs. But the truth is that Guatemala just barely met the standard.

And I fully agree with the Chairman on this issue and his views as it relates to this. We have one thought. Regardless of who wins the election next month, Guatemala must make a serious commitment to stop the flow of drugs. It must meet a higher standard if it hopes to be certified again.

And, finally, as Guatemala approaches the elections, I am concerned about reports of potential election fraud and intimidation of voters, and I urge all concerned to make sure that these are clean, fair, and open elections.

With reference to Cuba, the President recently announced a new Cuba Task Force. After 3 years of inaction, I believe it is too little too late. If the President, as he had promised during his election campaign, had lived up to his commitments to enforce the existing laws on Cuba, perhaps we would see more change in Cuba.

Instead, he has given the Cuban people and Cuban-Americans nothing more than empty promises and lip service. After President Clinton signed Helms-Burton into law, and was criticized by Republicans for waiving various titles within the law, President Bush has followed in his predecessor's steps.

He has continuously waived title 5, even though he said he would enforce the law. He has not enforced title 4, which denies visas to those major shareholders and CEOs who have participated in the confiscation of illegally seized property in Cuba, and are using it for their purposes. There has been no enforcement of title 4.

Wet foot/dry foot policy, this Administration has repatriated over 1,000 Cubans in the 2½, nearly 3 years of its Administration.

Stronger signals of Radio and Television Martí, absolutely not, and I could go on and on.

Everything that my colleagues and the President, when he was Candidate Bush excoriated Bill Clinton on, he has replicated exactly the same. Waive title 5, do not enforce title 4, wet foot/dry foot policy, everything is the same. Rhetoric is great. Now we are going to have a task force to figure out what we do after 3 years. That is rather ridiculous. We do not need more rhetoric on Cuba, we need definitive action and enforcement of the existing laws.

And lastly, it looks like the President is saying that he finally is ready to work with President Fox on immigration. We have heard noises from this Administration before on this. Time for talking is long past. It is in the national interest of the United States and in the national security of the United States, as well, to conclude a migration agreement with Mexico.

So, Mr. Chairman, we have a different view on the Administration's efforts in Latin America. To me, they appear to be deaf, dumb, and blind in this hemispheric policy. We need to see a change. Right now we have lost the battle in the hearts and minds of the Latin Americans. They must see a quality of life improved. They must see the benefits of stable democracy, and I believe the United States must be at the forefront of the battle for democracy and development, and must win back the hearts and minds of the Latin American people. It is in our national interest and our national security interest to do so, and I thank you for the time.

Mr. BALLENGER. Kind of reminds me of a quotation I once heard, "But Ms. Lincoln, what did you think of the show?"—"Not a great deal."

Let me introduce Roger Noriega. Roger Noriega was nominated by President George W. Bush for Assistant Secretary of State of the Western Hemisphere on March 24, 2003, and he was unanimously confirmed by the Senate.

Ambassador Noriega served as a U.S. permanent representative to the Organization of American States from 2001 to 2003. And before that he was a senior professional staff member for the Committee on Foreign Relations of the U.S. Senate.

From 1994 to 1997, he was a senior professional staff member for our Committee on International Relations.

Born in Wichita, Kansas in 1959, he attended Washburn University in Topeka, where he received a Bachelor of Arts Degree in 1981.

Welcome, Roger, and could you please proceed by summarizing your opening statement. Without objection, we will submit the full statement for the record.

STATEMENT OF THE HONORABLE ROGER F. NORIEGA, ASSISTANT SECRETARY OF STATE FOR WESTERN HEMISPHERE AFFAIRS, U.S. DEPARTMENT OF STATE

Mr. NORIEGA. Thank you very much, Mr. Chairman.

Mr. Chairman, I thank you and Members of this Subcommittee for the opportunity to discuss President Bush's Western Hemisphere strategy and vision. The President believes that the Americas are critically important to our security and to our well being as a nation. Our goal is to build an inter-American community bound together by a shared commitment to freedom, fortified by the rule of law, and prospering through free trade.

Geography we share creates natural economic relationships. Three of our top four foreign energy suppliers are in this hemisphere. United States exports to Latin America have increased by almost 100 percent over the last decade while our exports to the rest of the world have seen gains of less than 50 percent.

Canada and Mexico are our first and second largest trading partners in the world. U.S. leadership to expand global trade, to forge a Free Trade Area in the Americas and to reach bilateral agreements with willing partners will further strengthen this economic partnership.

Our economic relations in the Western Hemisphere are vital. Even if that were all we had a stake in the region, this region would demand our careful attention. But our political and security interests in the Americas are vital as well.

As we fight the global war on terror, it is imperative that we have strong, stable, democratic, neighbors working with us to secure our borders, and to defend our shared interests and values at home and abroad.

Mr. Chairman, allow me to discuss some of the challenges that we face in the region, noting that I will not be able to mention every country, but just address the challenges thematically.

Elected leaders in some countries in the region are grappling with persistent political, economic, social and sometimes ethnic tensions. Several countries are confronting costly threats to security—even in terms of narco-terrorism or violent crime—that undermine the rule of law and political stability.

We have yet to see a recovery from the poor economic performance in the region in 2002. Current economic growth rates are inadequate to generate sufficient jobs to keep up with the population growth, let alone address chronic poverty. Corruption and inefficiency have stunted economic development and spawned disenchantment with free market prescriptions.

All these factors have combined to stir popular dissatisfaction and, in some cases, even violent outbursts, which relatively weak institutions of government are hard-pressed to control. Five years ago, we could have spoken of improving governance and consolidating free markets; today, we must confront questions of governability and resist economic reversals.

The recent events in Bolivia, as you and Mr. Menendez have noted, underscore the challenges that we face in the region. As you know, President Sanchez de Lozada resigned last Friday in the face of organized violent protests. This is a real setback for the region, Mr. Chairman. We commend him for his commitment to democracy and to the prosperity of the Bolivian people which he demonstrated during his tenure. In conformity with Bolivia's constitution, Vice President Carlos Mesa was sworn in as President. The people of Bolivia and their leaders appear eager to end the strife and guarantee respect for democracy and the rule of law. Whatever the grievances, no Bolivian is better off under mob rule.

Mr. Chairman, having described the opportunities and challenges we face, albeit briefly, I would like to briefly describe also where we want to go with this hemisphere and how we plan to get there.

We want thriving economic partners that are democratic, stable, and prosperous. We want secure borders and cooperative neighbors, and we want a community of nations working together to advance common political and economic values in the world.

How do we get there? We will strengthen the roots and promote the benefits of democracy so that it serves all the interests of all of their people. Resilient and genuine democracy requires not just credible elections, but also administrations that govern effectively and defend the rights of all citizens.

We will help generate sustained economic growth by promoting trade, investment, and sound fiscal and monetary policies, investments in people, and policies that promote economic freedom.

Where market policies have fallen short of expectations, it is primarily due to man-made distortions, incomplete reform measures, corruption, over regulation, or discrimination. We will work to encourage countries to invest in their people so that they can all claim their fair share of economic opportunity and improve their quality of life. That is absolutely essential, Mr. Chairman, because it is not enough to just talk about generating income, but talking about building strong institutions that spread income, and more importantly, spread economic opportunity to people from all walks of life. Because if the poor people, the poor majority of people in the hemisphere cannot participate in the economic opportunity that is extended to others, than we will actually broaden the gap between rich and poor, and would make this economic experiment project unsustainable, and just as importantly, would not reach its full potential.

What tools will we use to pursue the objectives in the Americas? Strong U.S. leadership and engagement are essential to pursuing the strategy I have outlined. Trade and investment promotion is absolutely essential, but I would hasten to say it is not enough, and note that the income generated by the $240 billion that we import from Latin American and the Caribbean is 600 times the development assistance and Economic Support Funds that we have for the Western Hemisphere. So it is not enough, but it is absolutely indispensable to have trade and investment, and create climates in these countries where people want to do business and with which people want to trade.

United States development and security assistance can be decisive if it is used well. The ideal role for U.S. assistance is to help governments improve their own ability to meet basic social needs, deal with acute threats to security, and retool their economies so that their people can take full advantage of economic growth.

President Bush has proposed the Millennium Challenge Account to direct new resources to governments that are committed to governing justly, investing in their people, and promoting economic freedom. We urge Congress to approve a robust MCA program.

Mr. Chairman, we will continue to encourage the international financial institutions to support reform-oriented governments committed to implementing sound economic policies, and delivering lasting results to their people.

Finally, Mr. Chairman, multilateralism works in the Americas. The Organization of American States and the Summit of the Americas process are used by regional governments to revise common strategies and to put their political weight behind a comprehensive economic and political agenda.

An interim Summit of the Americas will bring the hemisphere's leaders together in Monterrey, Mexico next January to advance practical steps to encourage economic growth, reduce poverty, improve the quality of life of their citizens, and ensure more accountable, effective government.

In addition to our strategic goals which I have laid out here, there are some particular issues that I want to address and highlight very briefly.

Working with our neighbors to secure our borders has never been more important. As we work to tighten our security along with Mexico and Canada, we are taking special care to accommodate the dynamic commercial relationships which these countries, that are essential to our economic well being, bring. Also, we cannot neglect more than a dozen Caribbean states that see the mutual benefits of being good and stable neighbors to the United States.

We have to attack and continue to attack every link in the chain of illegal narcotics. It is absolutely crucial that we do that. For example, our support for the Colombian government's efforts is showing results. Last year we saw the first drop in Colombian coca cultivation in a decade of some 15 percent. Colombia's armed forces have stepped up a campaign to take back key national territory from the control of terrorist groups.

We must continue our support for Colombia and its neighbors. We cannot allow the terrorists and narcotics traffickers fleeing Colombia to regroup and restart their nefarious enterprises next door, the so-called "balloon effect." We must burst that balloon by continuing our work with Peru and Bolivia to ensure that they have the tools to prevent a resurgence of coca and heroin cultivation in their territory.

Promoting democracy in Venezuela, Haiti, and Cuba is a task that we share with our neighbors. We are committed to working with the OAS and others to achieve a "peaceful" democratic constitutional and electoral solution to Venezuela's impasse, as called for in OAS Resolution 833. The Government of Venezuela has a responsibility to ensure that all Venezuelans are able to exercise their constitutional rights by expressing their views through the media and at the ballot box.

With regard to Haiti, we have worked with our partners in the OAS to create a means by which confidence can be restored in the political process through small steps toward an election. The Haitian government has a unique responsibility to provide the secure environment necessary for free and fair elections, to uphold the rule of law, and to maintain public safety.

Regarding Cuba, President Bush has made it clear that the United States will not make any concessions to a dictatorship drawing its last breath. Just as important, he is committed to supporting the democratic struggle on the island with new creativity and vigor. He recently launched an Executive Branch commission to find ways to hasten the democratic transition, and to encourage broad and deep economic reform that will sweep away the vestiges of the Castro regime.

In conclusion, Mr. Chairman, although we must be realistic about the challenges in the Americas today, it is just as important to consider the tremendous progress that the people of the region have made in the least 10 to 15 years: Building governments that are more accountable and just, and economies that are more open in every respect.

But this progress is not irreversible. In many countries today dynamic democratic leaders recognize that free market-led policies are the formula for success in economic growth, but in too many cases there are others trying to take their countries down a very different path. For decades, the United States has supported political and economic reform, and we must respond urgently to consolidate and build on these hard-won gains before they slip away. To seize this opportunity, our policy must be forward looking, constructive, and optimistic. The steps we take in the next few months and years to defend democracy and to bolster broad-based economic growth in the Americas will be decisive in shoring up our key partners at a critical hour. It is essential to our economic and political interests that we do this.

Thank you very much, Mr. Chairman. I am pleased to answer any questions that you may have after Mr. Franco's opening statement. Thank you.

[The prepared statement of Mr. Noriega follows:]

PREPARED STATEMENT OF THE HONORABLE ROGER F. NORIEGA, ASSISTANT SECRETARY OF STATE FOR WESTERN HEMISPHERE AFFAIRS, U.S. DEPARTMENT OF STATE

I thank Chairmen Hyde and Ballenger and the members of the Committee for this opportunity to discuss the Bush Administration's Western Hemisphere strategy.

U.S. National Interest and Bush Administration Engagement in the Western Hemisphere

President Bush believes that the Americas are critically important to our security and to our well being as a nation. Our national interest in the Western Hemisphere is informed by the simple fact that it is our home. We have vital economic, political and security relationships with our neighbors. The President has demonstrated his commitment to the region from his first days in office, and he has articulated a clear vision for us to pursue.

Our goal is to build an inter-American community, bound together by the common value of freedom, fortified by the rule of law, and prospering through free trade.

A Shared Economic Destiny

The geography we share creates natural economic relationships. Three of our top four foreign energy suppliers are in this Hemisphere. U.S. exports to Latin America have increased by almost 100 percent over the past decade, while our exports to the rest of the world have seen gains of less than 50 percent. Canada and Mexico are our first- and second-largest trading partners. The envisioned "Free Trade Area of the Americas" will further strengthen and expand these partnerships.

The Administration has concluded a free trade agreement with Chile that had been sought for a decade. We are pleased that Congress acted quickly to approve that agreement. The President has initiated other trade agreements in the region. We are negotiating an FTA with Central America, and we have notified Congress of our intention to do the same with the Dominican Republic. In the meantime, we are working with all our partners in the region on the Free Trade Area of the Americas process.

When Uruguay faced the prospect of financial crisis, President Bush promptly provided a crucial billion-and-a-half dollar bridge loan. The U.S. also provided vital support to an IMF package for Brazil and the agreement between Argentina and the IMF, which, if fully implemented, will provide the conditions for robust, sustainable economic growth in that country.

Our economic relationships in the Western Hemisphere are vital, and if they were all that we had at stake here, the region would demand our careful attention. But our political and security interests in the Americas are vital as well. As we fight the Global War on Terror, it is imperative that we have strong, democratic neighbors working with us to secure our borders and defend our shared interests and values at home and aboard.

A Mutual Commitment to Democracy and Security

On September 11, 2001, the member states of the OAS signed the Inter-American Democratic Charter, a historic step that uniquely defines this region by its commitment to democratic principles. The Democratic Charter opens with a profound pledge—a pledge that we have made to our people and to one another: "The peoples of the Americas have a right to democracy, and the governments have an obligation to promote and defend it."

Today, cooperation on border security and law enforcement with Mexico and Canada has never been more comprehensive or successful. A new Inter-American Convention Against Terrorism entered into force recently. Soldiers from El Salvador, Nicaragua, Honduras and the Dominican Republic are with us in Iraq, working with our Armed Forces to secure that country and provide a better future and a democratic government for the long-suffering Iraqi people. We are very grateful for their help. Likewise in Colombia, we stand shoulder to shoulder with President Uribe and the democratic government against the combined forces of terrorist thugs and drug barons.

In the Americas, our shared values and essential commitment to democracy draw us together and move us to act in concert. It is clearly in our national interest that we strengthen our relationships with our neighbors and that we grow and prosper together. In the past twenty years, most of the countries in the region have made great progress in building democratic systems of government, but it must be said that, today, the Hemisphere is troubled.

Challenges

Elected leaders in many countries are grappling with persistent political, economic, social, and, in some cases, ethnic problems. Several countries are confronting costly threats to security—either in terms of narco-terrorism or violent crime—that undermine the rule of law.

We are not seeing a recovery from the poor economic performance in the region in 2002. Current economic growth rates are inadequate to generate sufficient jobs for growing populations, let alone address chronic poverty. Corruption and inefficiency have stunted economic development and spawned disenchantment with "free market" prescriptions.

All these factors have combined to stir popular dissatisfaction and, in some cases, violent outbursts, which relatively weak institutions of government are hard-pressed to control. Five years ago, we could speak of improving governance and consolidating free markets; today, we must confront questions of "governability" and resist economic reversals.

The recent events in Bolivia underscore the challenges that we face in the region. As you know, President Sanchez de Lozada resigned last Friday. We commend him for his commitment to democracy and to the welfare of Bolivia during his tenure. In conformity with Bolivia's constitution, Vice-President Carlos Mesa was sworn in as President.

The Unites States deeply regrets the loss of life resulting from the violence of the past week in Bolivia. The people of Bolivia and their leaders share a responsibility to end the strife and guarantee respect for human life and the rule of law. The United States stands ready, along with the members of the Organization of American States and other democracies, to assist the Bolivian people and their government as they undertake the essential task of repairing their national institutions.

U.S. Objectives and Strategy

Our objectives for the Western Hemisphere are clear. We want thriving economic partners that are democratic, stable, and prosperous. We want secure borders and cooperative neighbors. And we want a community of nations working together to advance common political and economic values in the world. President Bush's policy is to work with our partners in the region to make democracy better serve every citizen; to generate economic growth through free trade, sound macroeconomic policies that encourage economic freedom; and to invest in the well-being of people from all walks of life.

We will strengthen the roots and promote the benefits of democracy so that it serves the interests of all people. Resilient and genuine democracy requires not just credible electoral systems, but also administrations that govern effectively and defend the rights of all citizens. Real democracy requires effective legislatures, independent judiciaries, professional media, principled political parties, and militaries that respect their role in a democratic society. These institutions—as well as checks and balances among branches of government—help prevent abuses of power and popular dissatisfaction before they escalate into a crisis. I hasten to note that this democratic model, far from being imposed by any country, is enshrined in the Inter-American Democratic Charter that was signed by all active OAS member states.

We will help generate sustained economic growth by promoting trade, investment, and sound fiscal and monetary policies, investments in people, and policies that promote economic freedom. President Bush put it emphatically when he said, "Open trade is not just an economic opportunity, it is a moral imperative. . . . Open trade helps us all adhere to values that we share." Our economic engagement through trade and investment is a crucial tool in helping our friends, and we are putting it to work.

The Bush Administration helped launch the Doha Round in the World Trade Organization, secured Trade Promotion Authority from Congress, completed negotiations with Chile on a free trade accord, began trade talks with Central America and campaigned for the expanded Andean Trade Promotion and Drug Eradication Act. We hope all our region's leaders see trade as an indispensable tool for their own nations' economic and social development. We remain committed to the FTAA process. We will also explore opportunities for other Free Trade Agreements, beginning with the Dominican Republic.

Where market policies have fallen short of expectations, it is primarily due to man-made distortions, incomplete reform measures, corruption, over-regulation, or discrimination. A thriving, sturdy economy must be built on the bedrock of respect for the rule of law and property rights, coherent macroeconomic policies—including fiscally responsible public budgets, fair tax codes, and other economic reforms that will provide a basis for growth.

We will encourage countries to "invest in people" so they can claim their fair share of economic opportunity and improve their quality of life. Hand-in-hand with our commitments to govern better and to retool our economies, we must pursue, as President Bush has called it, "prosperity with a purpose"—where people are above the bottom line.

Statist or corrupt economic models that hoard opportunity or dole out state-sponsored privileges to a chosen few cannot keep up in the 21st century. Experience the world over has shown that economic growth is the *sina qua non* of poverty reduction. In turn, the resources generated by growth must be used to make sustained social investments in quality education, adequate health and nutritional care, basic sanitation, and personal security.

Such social programs are more than altruistic: investing in human capital is good business . . . because economies cannot begin to grow fast enough to generate needed jobs—let alone to defeat extreme poverty—unless all our people have the tools and the opportunity to pull their own weight. Above all, our social policies must demonstrate that we are committed, not to short-term, unsustainable handouts, but to growth with equity in which every citizen can become a stakeholder in their economy.

Policy Tools

What tools will we use to pursue our objectives in the Americas?

Strong U.S. leadership and engagement are essential to pursuing this strategy. We must continue to demonstrate energy and idealism to reassure our neighbors—including skeptics and critics—that the United States is a principled and trustworthy partner and that we want to grow together in every sense. To do this, we must make our policies clear and consistent, and we must treat our neighbors with respect.

U.S. development and security assistance can be decisive, if it is used well. The ideal role for U.S. assistance is to help governments improve their own ability to meet basic social needs, deal with acute threats to security, and retool their economies so that their people can take full advantage of economic growth. Current USG programs in the region include promoting economic growth and trade capacity, strengthening democracy and the rule of law, improving the quality and ensuring access to education and health services.

President Bush has proposed the Millennium Challenge Account (MCA) to direct new resources to governments that are committed to governing justly, investing in their people, and promoting economic freedom. This infusion of new assistance to reform-minded governments tackling systemic poverty is a wise and potentially decisive investment of U.S. aid, and the Bush Administration urges Congress to approve a robust MCA program.

International lenders must play a constructive role. Governments in the Americas need to pursue sound macroeconomic policies essential for maintaining access to private capital markets. We will continue to encourage the international financial institutions to support reform-oriented governments committed to implementing sound economic policies and delivering lasting results to their people.

We will work directly with the countries in the region to strengthen their economic policies so that they can reap the benefits of macroeconomic stability and faster economic growth. This year, our Treasury Department and the Brazilian Finance Ministry launched the U.S.-Brazil Group for Growth, a bilateral forum that brings together high-level economic officials from both our countries with the goal of developing economic strategies to raise economic growth in both countries. We have also made great strides through the U.S.-Mexico Partnership for Prosperity to lower the costs of remittances sent to Mexico and strengthen Mexico's financial sector.

Finally, *Multilateralism works in the Americas.* The Summit of the Americas meetings have been used by heads of government to consult with one another and to put their political weight behind a visionary and comprehensive agenda of initiatives advancing common interests. We support enthusiastically plans for a special summit of leaders early next year to maintain momentum behind our shared agenda. The OAS mechanisms to promote democracy, address terrorism, the problem of drugs in the hemisphere, and political crises have been important foreign policy tools.

Several Key Concerns

In addition to our strategic goals, there are several emergent issues that require our immediate attention.

Working with our neighbors to secure our borders has never been more important. The United States is truly blessed with good neighbors—Canada, Mexico, and the

Caribbean—and strengthening these partnerships is a high priority. Since September 11, 2001, the necessity of securing our common borders with Canada and Mexico has commanded much greater attention and resources. As we work to tighten our security, we must take care to accommodate the dynamic commercial relationship with these countries that is essential to our economic well-being.

In tending to security close to home, we should recall that the Caribbean forms our "third border." If we are going to forge a genuine community in the Americas, then we cannot neglect more than a dozen island states simply because their economies and populations are small. Moreover—despite their democratic traditions and institutions—they remain especially vulnerable and present inviting targets for smugglers of illegal drugs and migrants, money launderers, and other criminal elements that mean to do us harm.

Attacking every link in the chain of illegal narcotics trafficking is crucial, beginning with driving down drug consumption here at home. We must remember that the profits from illegal drug sales support violent criminal gangs and terrorist groups.

The Bush Administration has made a robust new commitment to attacking the cocaine and heroin trade at one of its most important sources, in Colombia and the rest of the Andes. President Uribe of Colombia has requested our help with training, equipment and intelligence support. We have responded, providing Colombia with almost $3 billion in assistance since 2000. The Colombians have matched our assistance by redoubling their efforts. President Uribe has boosted security spending, increased the number of military and police, and mounted a concerted effort to re-establish state presence throughout Colombia's territory.

Our support for the Colombian government's efforts is showing results. The drug eradication campaign produced the first drop in Colombian coca cultivation in a decade, some 15 percent. "Carabinero" teams have begun policing close to 150 municipalities that previously lacked a police presence. At the same time, Colombia's armed forces have stepped up the campaign to take back key national territory from the control of terrorist groups. The FARC and ELN are now on the defensive, and Uribe has successfully pressured paramilitary forces to come to the table to discuss disarmament and demobilization.

We remain confident that President Uribe shares our fundamental commitment to protecting human rights. I would note that during the past year we have seen a sharp drop in Colombia's murder rate, including political killings, a significant decline in kidnappings, a marked drop in violence against labor leaders and a decline in the number of new internal displacements.

We must continue our support for Colombia and its neighbors. We cannot allow the terrorists and narcotics traffickers fleeing Colombia to regroup and restart their nefarious enterprises next door, the so-called "balloon effect." We must pop that balloon. We will continue to work with Peru and Bolivia to ensure they have the tools to prevent a resurgence of coca cultivation in their territory. Eradication must be complemented by intelligence-driven law enforcement that dismantles criminal gangs, dries up money laundering, seizes assets, and interdicts contraband headed for our shores. We will continue our alternative development activities to discourage *campesinos* from returning to illicit crops, mindful that the reach of these programs also depends on the security climate. Moreover, our experience has taught us that fighting drugs and terrorism is not only *compatible* with respecting human rights, the two goals are mutually reinforcing.

Promoting democracy in Venezuela, Haiti, and Cuba is a task that we share with our neighbors. The regional consensus in favor of representative democracy has produced a strong framework for defending our democratic values. The Inter-American Democratic Charter defines the essential elements of democracy and commits all nations to promote and defend it. We have an opportunity to do so in Venezuela, Haiti, and Cuba.

We are committed to working with the OAS and others to achieve a "peaceful, democratic, constitutional and electoral solution" to Venezuela's political impasse as called for in OAS resolution 833. It is critical that the government of Venezuela and the opposition honor their commitments under the May 29 accord. In particular, the government of Venezuela has a special responsibility to ensure that all Venezuelans are able to exercise their constitutional rights to freedom of association and expression.

We will continue to support the OAS, the Carter Center and the UN's Democracy Program's efforts both individually and as a member of the Group of Friends of the OAS Secretary General. We are also committed to providing technical support to Venezuela's electoral authorities, if they so request.

With regard to Haiti, we have worked with our partners in the OAS to create a means by which confidence can be restored in the political process. OAS Resolution

822 is the result that effort, and the United States encourages all sides in Haiti to follow the road-map it has outlined. President Aristide, as the leader of his country, has a unique responsibility to provide the secure environment necessary for free and fair elections, to uphold the law and maintain public safety. Violence has no place in settling political disputes in a democracy.

It is my fervent hope that the good people of Cuba are studying the Democratic Charter, because it represents a path to their reintegration into a free Hemisphere. President Bush has made it clear that the United States will not make any concessions to the Castro dictatorship in Cuba. Just as important, he is committed to supporting the democratic struggle on the island with new creativity and vigor. To that end, we must redouble our bilateral and multilateral efforts to bring an end to the dictatorship and to encourage broad and deep economic reform that will sweep away the vestiges of the regime.

The recent ruthless crackdown on dissidents and independent journalists demonstrates that the Castro regime is threatened by the growing internal opposition groups and by their expanding network of international support. The inter-American community should do more than wish for Cuba's freedom, we should work together like never before to make it a reality.

To enhance the energy security of the United States, and of the Hemisphere as a whole, we should increase the accessibility of energy supplies from sources closer to home. President Bush's National Energy Policy calls for greater integration with our NAFTA partners, bolstering investment in Venezuela and Brazil, and invigorating the Hemispheric Energy Initiative. We should treat this initiative as one of our highest priorities.

Our approach should focus on reliable, environmentally balanced, and affordable access to energy. Vast oil and gas reserves exist in the Americas. For example, Trinidad and Tobago already is a small but strategically significant supplier of liquefied natural gas to the United States and is poised to increase its exports substantially in the next few years. New technologies to exploit oil sands will boost Canada's already significant petroleum reserves. An increased supply of energy in the Americas not only will contribute significantly to the economic growth of the United States, but it will also improve the standard of living of people in the region and bolster economic and political stability.

Conclusion

Although we must be realistic about the challenges in the Americas today, it is just as important to consider the tremendous progress that the people of the region have made in just the last 10–15 years, building governments that are more accountable and just and economies that are more open in every respect. This progress is not irreversible. In many countries today, dynamic, democratic leaders recognize that free-market led policies are the formula for success. But, in too many cases, there are others trying to take their countries down a very different path. For decades, the United States has supported political and economic reform, and we must respond urgently to consolidate and build on these hard-won gains before they slip away.

To seize this opportunity, our policy must be forward-looking, constructive, and optimistic. The steps we take in the next few months and years to defend democracy and to bolster broad-based economic growth in the Americas will be decisive in shoring-up our key partners at a critical hour. It is essential to our economic and political interests to do this.

The strategy I have outlined today is one that enjoys considerable support in the region. It also enjoys strong bipartisan backing here at home, which is reflected in this Congress. As someone who has spent a decade working directly for Members of Congress, I recognize that your active engagement in these issues is not merely helpful; it is indispensable.

As President George W. Bush has stated, "This hemisphere is on the path of reform, and our nations travel it together. We share a vision—a partnership of strong and equal and prosperous countries, living and trading in freedom. . . . We'll maintain our vision, because it unleashes the possibilities of every society and recognizes the dignity of every person." In pursuit of this vision, our goals are clear, our strategy is sound, and our policy tools are at work.

Mr. BALLENGER. Now, let me introduce my good friend, Adolfo Franco. Adolfo was sworn in on January 31, 2002, as Assistant Administrator, Bureau for Latin America and the Caribbean of the U.S. Agency for International Development, USAID.

Before joining USAID, Franco served as Counsel to the Majority on the House International Relations Committee. From 1999 to 2000, he was President of the Inter-American Foundation. Adolfo was born in Cuba, his Bachelor's and Master's degrees are in history from the University of Northern Iowa, and his law degree from Creighton University School of Law.

Welcome back, Adolfo. Could you please proceed by summarizing your opening statement? And without objection, we will submit the full statement for the record. Thank you.

STATEMENT OF THE HONORABLE ADOLFO A. FRANCO, ASSISTANT ADMINISTRATOR FOR LATIN AMERICA AND THE CARIBBEAN, U.S. AGENCY FOR INTERNATIONAL DEVELOPMENT

Mr. FRANCO. Thank you, Mr. Chairman. It is really a wonderful pleasure to be back before the Committee. I know we have a lot of challenging questions ahead of us, but it is always a pleasure to come before the House International Relations Committee.

Last February is the last time you had me up here to talk about the challenges that we are facing in the region, so I would like to just take a few minutes today to update you on the President's vision and the program that we are implementing in the Western Hemisphere to support the President's foreign policy objectives as articulated by Secretary Noriega.

As the Secretary has noted, this region, and I do not think there is any disagreement with anyone on this room, is extremely vital to the prosperity and security of the United States. Secretary Noriega stated, and I fully concur, that the ideal role for U.S. assistance is to help governments improve their own ability to meet basic social needs with emphasis on education and how to deal with acute threats to security so they are able to retool their economies and enable their people to take full advantage of economic growth.

And these are indeed the areas where USAID programs work today. At USAID, we focus on democracy and anti-corruption initiatives, trade-led economic growth programs, counternarcotics efforts that provide alternatives to rural farmers, and reforms that encourage governments to invest additional resources in basic education and health as the President of the United States called for last year before the Inter-American Development Bank when he announced his visionary Millennium Challenge Account.

As the distinguished Members of the Committee are only too aware, Latin America and the Caribbean, however, face ongoing development challenges that threaten the gains we have made in democracy, and actually threaten the national security and economy of the United States.

Now, I would just like to articulate, and I think Mr. Menendez did a very thorough job of doing this, the areas we are very concerned with, and they have to do with contracting economic growth rates in the region, extensive poverty, unemployment, skewed income distribution unparalleled in the world, crime and lawlessness, a thriving narcotics industry and trade, and a deteriorating natural resource base. These are the things that continue to undermine the stability of the region.

In addition, the risk of HIV/AIDS and drug resistant tuberculosis on our borders threatens the United States very directly.

All of this has led to a decline in the confidence of citizens in their democratically-elected governments as they are unable to provide the necessary security and prosperity, and therefore that confidence in democracy in the region is in some quarters beginning to wane. The best example is, of course, what happened in Bolivia last week as articulated by the Assistant Secretary.

In order to address these challenges, USAID's programs work in three broad categories which I would like to discuss: Democracy and good governance, economic growth, and investing in people.

Democracy and good governance, something that USAID achieves by working on anti-corruption, or seeks to achieve by working on anti-corruption programs, supporting the rule of law, municipal governance, and strengthening of civil society organizations.

For example, USAID provides assistance to devise national and local anti-corruption plans throughout the hemisphere.

In Ecuador, an anti-corruption commission created with USAID support has now the investigative authority to uncover cases of corruption. This is the first instance in that country that an entity, a government agency, has had that authority.

USAID works to strengthen judicial and legal systems and helps expand access to alternative dispute resolution for the poor and other marginalized citizens through a growing network of community-based centers.

On economic growth, President Bush, Secretary Powell and the USAID Administrator, Andrew Natsios, as well as the U.S. Trade Representative, Ambassador Bob Zoellick, have all stated that trade and investment, and I concur, are essential to economic growth and poverty reduction. USAID supports the enactment of legal, policy, and regulatory reforms that promote trade and investment as the long-term engines for economic growth.

USAID support for trade capacity building has increased substantially in the last 2 years of this Administration, and USAID plans to continue to increase that support in the coming years.

The failure of trade ministers to reach agreement at the recent Cancun WTO Ministerial Conference only serves to reinforce the importance of USAID's work during the trade negotiation process. USAID is helping to promote the completion of the United States-Central American Trade Agreement, known as CAFTA, and is seeking to promote the eventual Free Trade Area of the Americas agreement known as FTAA, and fully supports the recently announced Hemispheric Cooperation Program to achieve these goals.

In this area of trade capacity, let me just say for one moment these are the things that bring about confidence in democracy. Trade capacity means building, as Secretary Noriega has said, building institutions at the national and local level, being able to respect the rule of law, sanctity of contracts, and an ability for a society to function as we know it.

Other examples of USAID programs in the area of broad-based economic growth include a region-wide rural economic diversification program to enable farmers to access new and growing markets in the developed world, and to channel private remittances into useful investments among others.

Investing in people is what the President has articulated as a fundamental principle of his Administration and his foreign policy. And in our bureau at USAID we have done everything to promote the President's priorities of health and education for our region.

In health, we have made significant progress in raising vaccination coverage and reducing or eliminating major childhood diseases such as measles.

Also, because of USAID assistance, affected countries are now more willing to discuss the HIV/AIDS program than they were 2 years ago. This is particularly relevant in our hemisphere as the Caribbean has the second highest rate of HIV/AIDS prevalence in the world.

The USAID education and training programs work to improve the poor state of the region's public education systems. The President announced the Centers of Excellence in Teacher Training as his presidential initiative that now trains hundreds of primary school instructors in effective techniques for teaching reading skills throughout the region.

Now, Mr. Chairman, I would like to outline particularly difficult development challenges that we are facing in the Western Hemisphere.

Prior to the most recent unrest, USAID had been working with the government of Bolivia to address its economic and fiscal problems. As you are aware, the new cycle of conflict that developed in late September and early October as worker unions, coca farmers and others united to prevent the sale of Bolivia's underground gas deposits escalated more rapidly than we had thought.

A month of increasingly violent protests led to the death of scores of people from clashes between protesters and the military, and has forced President Sanchez de Lozada to resign. Along with our colleagues at the State Department, we are monitoring the situation very closely and reviewing our policy and programs in Bolivia in light of these recent developments, and doing everything possible to support the new government.

However, despite the recent upheaval in Bolivia, this is a country where there has been successful cooperation in our counternarcotics efforts. Due to a strong eradication effort, coca production in Bolivia has declined an estimated 70 percent since 1998 alone. USAID's alternative development programs were instrumental in making this a success, as these programs provide poor farmers with choices other than coca with an emphasis on small business development and the construction of infrastructure projects to help increase access to markets for rural producers.

In Colombia, the threat of narco-trafficking continues to endanger the social and economic fabric of Colombian society and poses a direct threat to the United States. President Alvaro Uribe has done much to combat narco-trafficking, but a lack of state presence in large portions of the country has allowed both illegal narcotics production and armed drug dealing terrorist organizations to flourish.

USAID programs in Colombia focus in these areas. Our alternative development activities provide economic alternatives to coca, and we again provide infrastructure and other development in Putamayo and other affected areas so that poor farmers and others will have an opportunity and an alternative to illicit activities.

In Colombia, our judicial reform efforts also include a system of community-based legal services know as the Casas de Justicia, which provide for alternative dispute resolution and other legal services to the urban and rural poor who have been marginalized and not part of that society for far too long.

The USAID also assists Colombia's internally displaced people, the only internally displaced people in this hemisphere, and protects the human rights workers and others who are doing everything possible to prevent future massacres and forced displacements.

In Haiti, 2 decades of poor governance and economic mismanagement have brought that country to a near standstill. The United States is currently the largest donor in Haiti and provides nearly $70 million to Haiti, including large amounts to the Haitian people, including large amounts of food under the P.L. 480 Title II program. USAID also works with Haiti's human rights community, works to strengthen Haitian independent media, and works with the Haitian Diaspora to find ways to foster democracy, promote economic growth in that country, and reach a political settlement to the impasse that has eluded that country for the past 2 years.

In Venezuela, the United States is a strong supporter of a resolution to the Venezuelan political crisis. Over the past year, USAID has provided over 70 grants worth $2 million to address the Venezuelan conflict. These grants provide dialogue between the government and the opposition, often at the local level. USAID grantees help political parties establish a stronger role in the country and we are seeking to have them regain the trust of the electorate.

The USAID programs also monitor the status and operation of the judicial system and its ongoing activities, and works with the Venezuelan Congress to improve legislation and laws.

Mr. Menendez referred to Guatemala. As the Members of the Committee are well aware, Guatemala has recently improved its cooperation with United States antinarcotics efforts, and was recertified by the President.

Nonetheless, as noted by Mr. Menendez, corruption, organized crime, and weak enforcement of the law have made it difficult to promote democracy effectively in that country.

To combat these threats, USAID has been helping Guatemala's judicial sector strengthen its ability to combat corruption at every level.

In Colombia, USAID supports 27 justice centers that help local communities, churches and governments access police, prosecutors, judges, and public defenders in an effort to fight crime, ensure respect for human rights, and mediate dispute.

While Mr. Menendez and other Members of the Committee, and my testimony as well, have highlighted many of the challenges and difficulties we face, I do want to highlight some of the positive developments as well.

As Secretary Noriega points out, the signing of the Inter-American Democracy Charter and the Inter-American Convention Against Corruption—these are documents of the Organization of

American States—demonstrate a commitment to good governance by Latin American and Caribbean countries.

Nicaragua is an example of a country that is doing everything possible to curb government corruption, and other countries such as Mexico have made important commitments to reduce official corruption. Elections in the past in Jamaica, Brazil, Ecuador, and Colombia have all been judged to be free and fair, and there are many examples where we are working to build on these positive developments by continuing to support the institutions of democracy that the citizens of these countries have a right to expect.

Mr. Chairman, President Bush and Secretary Powell have said that no region of the world is more important to the long-term prosperity and security of the United States than Latin America and the Caribbean. Nowhere else do events—such as the political instability we witnessed in Bolivia, the terrorism that we have in the Andean region, drug trafficking in South America and the Caribbean, and the economic crisis of the region—have such a profound effect on our national interest and the well-being of the American people.

Therefore, USAID programs in the region are pivotal to supporting the foreign policy of the United States which is, as Secretary Noriega has articulated, to promote sustainable economic growth, strengthen democracy, the rule of law, and provide improved access to health care and education while combatting illegal narcotics.

Much remains to be done, but we at USAID working with the State Department will continue to promote a more secure, democratic and prosperous Latin America and Caribbean region for the benefit not only of the peoples of the region, but for the American people and the international community as a whole.

Mr. Chairman, I would be very pleased to answer any questions that you or the other Members of this distinguished Committee might have for me.

[The prepared statement of Mr. Franco follows:]

PREPARED STATEMENT OF THE HONORABLE ADOLFO A. FRANCO, ASSISTANT ADMINISTRATOR FOR LATIN AMERICA AND THE CARIBBEAN, U.S. AGENCY FOR INTERNATIONAL DEVELOPMENT

Mr. Chairman, Members of the Committee, it is a pleasure again to have the opportunity to appear before the Subcommittee on the Western Hemisphere of the House International Relations Committee. The last time that I appeared before this Subcommittee, in February of this year, I took the opportunity to discuss with you how USAID's Bureau for Latin America and the Caribbean (LAC) is implementing the President's vision for the Western Hemisphere. Today I would like to update you on the strategic priorities, country and regional programs, and new initiatives of the LAC bureau, and brief you on how USAID continues to support the President's foreign policy in a region so critical to the prosperity and security of the United States.

As Assistant Secretary Noriega has stated, "The ideal role for U.S. assistance is to help governments improve their own ability to meet basic social needs, with emphasis on education and health, deal with acute threats to security, and retool their economies so that their people can take full advantage of economic growth." These are precisely the areas where USAID programs work today, with focus on democracy and anti-corruption initiatives, trade-led economic growth, counternarcotics programs that provide alternatives to rural farmers, and social sector reform to encourage governments to invest additional resources in basic education and health.

The recent approval of the joint State Department/USAID Strategic Planning Framework provides a basis to improve the impact and coordination of our programs. Further, Secretary Powell's introduction to the joint strategy states that USAID's development programs are fully in line with foreign policy in support of the President's National Security Strategy, a work to "create a more secure, democratic, and prosperous world for the benefit of the American people and the international community."

STRATEGIC FOCUS

As discussed in USAID's recently published report *Foreign Aid in the National Interest*, one of the most significant lessons we have learned in development assistance is that governance, policies, institutions and political leadership, and not resources contributed from outside, matter most. The LAC Bureau is committed to using our resources in the most effective way possible, including consideration of government performance and commitment. This includes allocating additional resources to countries which enjoy responsible governance and accountability. We continue to recognize that, ultimately, each country has primary responsibility for its own development.

USAID's strategic priorities in the LAC region are to: (1) help promote democracy and combat corruption; (2) support trade-led economic growth; and (3) reduce narcotics trafficking. These key themes give paramount importance to the implementation of sound policies that address the principal constraints to development, with the overarching goal of furthering the overall foreign policy agenda.

The LAC Bureau's strategy is being carried out through three major programmatic and management approaches, one for each of the three sub-regions in LAC: the Central American and Mexico (CAM) Regional Strategy focuses on trade-led development and the Central America Free Trade Agreement (CAFTA); the Andean Counterdrug Initiative focuses on counternarcotics; and programs in the Caribbean region combat HIV/AIDS and promote growth and diversification in small island economies. Because countries within each of the sub-regions face similar key development challenges, LAC is developing regional strategies to provide a single framework for both regional and country-level programs. I am pleased to announce that USAID missions in Central America and Mexico have already launched a new joint regional strategy focused on three goals: transparent governance, economic freedom, and social investment.

In addition to country-specific and regional activities, USAID in the LAC region is addressing critical transnational issues such as HIV/AIDS, a deteriorating natural resource base, trafficking in persons, and inefficient education systems. USAID is also committed to mobilizing resources from and fostering alliances with U.S. public and private sector.

CONTINUING CHALLENGES

The Latin America and Caribbean region faces ongoing development challenges that threaten the national security and economy of the United States. Contracting economic growth rates, extensive poverty, unemployment, skewed income distribution, crime and lawlessness, a thriving narcotics industry and a deteriorating natural resource base continue to undermine the stability of the region. The risks of HIV/AIDS and drug-resistant tuberculosis on our borders also threaten the population of the United States. Civil unrest threatens democracy in Bolivia, and political instability in Venezuela and Haiti continues. Increasingly, citizens' confidence in the ability of democratically elected governments to provide security and prosperity is waning.

The region's GDP shrank by approximately 0.8% in 2002. This represents the region's worst economic performance since 1983. In 2002 inflation reached 12% after eight years of steady decline. Mediocre economic performance has caused per capita income in LAC countries to decline significantly since 1998, while poverty has increased. These difficulties have brought discontent and political turbulence, shaken citizens' faith in democracy, investment priorities, social sector policies, and the benefits of a decade of liberal reforms. The effects in the poorest countries, such as Haiti, and even in regions of countries with generally solid economic performance, such as northeast Brazil, have been more disheartening.

Still, it is important not to portray the region in an entirely negative light. Overall GDP is expected to grow by 1.5% in 2003, and inflation is on track to return to 8% to 9% this year. The Argentine economy is expected to grow by at least 5% by the end of this year. Chile, Peru, and the Dominican Republic are expected to show strong growth in 2003, with expansion of 3% or more, assuming that the slowdown in the United States abates and strong growth resumes. Countries that have adopted sound fiscal policies and oriented their economies toward foreign investment and rules-based trade under the World Trade Organization (WTO) have tended to resist the recent downturn and stand to benefit more from the nascent world and U.S. recovery.

PROGRAM INITIATIVES

The LAC Bureau is responding to Presidential Initiatives with a special emphasis on those that have implications for the Western Hemisphere. The initiatives are: the Central America Free Trade Agreement; Global Fund to Fight AIDS, TB and Malaria; Emergency Plan for AIDS Relief; Mother and Child HIV Prevention; Initiative for a New Cuba, Centers for Excellence in Teacher Training; Global Climate Change; and Initiative Against Illegal Logging. These initiatives fall into three broad program areas that I will now discuss: Democracy and Governance, Sustainable Economic Growth, and Investing in People.

Democracy and Good Governance

While support for democracy remains solid in the LAC region, popular disillusionment with governments that cannot reduce poverty, corruption, or crime is growing. Many countries' democracies remain fragile and are in need of reinforcing the institutional building blocks of democracy. USAID is working to strengthen democracy through programs in anti-corruption, strengthening rule of law, municipal governance, and civil society strengthening.

Anti-corruption programs emphasize prevention, citizen oversight, and building the capacity of countries to attack weak governance, entrenched political institutions, and poor public sector management. USAID provides assistance to citizens groups and non-governmental organizations to devise national and local anti-corruption plans and to monitor the dealings of public officials and government agencies. USAID supports local initiatives to establish special commissions and investigative units to expose and prosecute cases of corruption by public officials. For example, in Ecuador, the Anti-Corruption Commission has the investigative authority to uncover cases of corruption. In Nicaragua, USAID provides assistance to improve the capacity of the Attorney General's Office to tackle high-profile corruption cases against the former government.

Recent increases in crime and violence are consistently cited by citizens as one of their primary concerns. The endemic problems of impunity for violent crime, corruption, and money laundering, and narcotics-related crime undercut social and economic growth in many LAC countries. USAID is responding in more than a dozen countries in the Hemisphere by providing direct assistance for modernization of the justice sectors.

The implementation of new Criminal Procedure Codes and other criminal justice system reforms, developed and enacted over the last decade with USAID support in Nicaragua, Honduras, Guatemala, El Salvador, Bolivia, Colombia, and the Dominican Republic, is introducing profound changes as countries move from written inquisitorial justice systems toward oral adversarial systems. USAID is helping other countries, such as Peru, to transition to such systems and introduce reforms that will make judicial selection more transparent and improve oversight of the courts in order to increase accountability. In Colombia and Guatemala, USAID is expanding access to alternative dispute resolution and other legal services to millions of marginalized citizens through a growing network of community-based centers.

As a key element of the justice system, it is essential that the police do their jobs responsibly and that there is trust between the police and the communities in which they work. Section 660 restrictions of the FAA limit our ability to work on critical security issues such as community policing, which is increasingly integral to development in many LAC countries. However, specific legislative authorization has allowed USAID to initiate a community policing program in Jamaica and to continue a successful program in El Salvador. The program in El Salvador is part of a larger law enforcement institutional development program conducted in cooperation with the Departments of State and Justice. [dsb1]

USAID-supported training and technical assistance helps strengthen the capacity of national and local governments to demonstrate that responsible leaders can deliver benefits to communities. With the direct election of local mayors and the devolution of authority to municipalities, USAID is helping citizens and elected leaders devise community development plans that respond to local needs and generate growth. In fourteen countries, USAID helped mayors establish transparent accounting and financial management procedures with USAID assistance to create the framework for greater revenue generation for roads, schools, health centers, and job creation. In turn, citizens monitor the use of public funds and devise "social audits" in countries such as the Dominican Republic and Bolivia to track spending in accordance with local development plans in order to keep officials accountable to the public.

Economic Growth

Sustained development depends on market-based economies, sound monetary and fiscal policies, sound management of natural resources, and increased trade and investment. We are mindful of the critical need to continue these efforts and build on our experiences in order to encourage further economic development. As President Bush, Secretary Powell, USTR Ambassador Zoellick, and Administrator Natsios have all said, trade and investment are essential to economic growth and poverty reduction. Without an increase in trade and investment, the region's substantial development gains will be put at risk, and hemispheric stability could falter. USAID is supporting LAC countries to enact legal, policy and regulatory reforms that promote trade and investment as the engines for economic growth.

USAID support for trade capacity building has increased substantially in recent years, and USAID plans to continue to increase support for trade capacity building. The failure of trade ministers to reach agreement at the recent Cancun WTO Ministerial conference only serves to reinforce the importance of USAID's work in the trade negotiation process. As I stated in Cancun at a press conference with U.S. Trade Representative Ambassador Robert Zoellick, USAID is convinced that assistance for trade capacity building, when combined with a strong commitment to openness and reform on the part of our developing country partners, is one of the U.S. Government's most powerful tools for promoting economic growth and poverty reduction.

In August 2002, President Bush signed the Trade Act of 2002, and launched the Presidential Initiative on CAFTA. In January 2003, I participated with Ambassador Zoellick in the inauguration of negotiations for the CAFTA which are expected to conclude by December of this year. USAID supported trade capacity building and civil society outreach efforts in the region included technical training on trade issues for government officials that will allow the Dominican Republic to participate in CAFTA. As part of this process, USAID worked closely with other institutions such as the Inter-American Development Bank, the Organization of American States, and the Economic Commission for Latin American and the Caribbean to assist each Central American country to prepare a national trade capacity building strategy in support of its participation in the CAFTA process. In addition, CAFTA will include an environmental chapter under which USAID will assist CAFTA partners to strengthen their environmental management and institutional capacity.

I recently attended the inaugural session of the donors' roundtable under the FTAA's Hemispheric Cooperation Program on October 14–15. USAID fully supports this program, along with the Office of the U.S. Trade Representative, and is committed to helping countries reach their goals under this program.

Negotiation of the Free Trade Area of the Americas (FTAA) agreement will continue to be of the highest importance in the future. USAID has also been working in partnership with the region's smaller economies to help them to participate effectively in the global trading system by building trade negotiating capacity, developing markets, and providing assistance for business development. In response to requests from country governments, USAID will assist governments to comply with the "rules of trade" such as sanitary/phytosanitary measures, customs reform, and intellectual property rights. For example, as a result of a USAID-supported program in Jamaica, which is led by the private sector and provides specific information to private and public sector leaders on the benefits of free trade, the Jamaican private sector now better understands the potential benefits of free trade and has become a stronger advocate of the FTAA.

The U.S. Government is updating the President's Third Border Initiative (TBI) to respond to critical security needs in the Caribbean, and we have also added a trade component to strengthen the capacity and competitiveness of Caribbean countries. We will build on modest trade activities already underway for several years, in the Caribbean, a sub-region with many small island economies which lack diverse sources of income. When launched in 2001, TBI aimed to strengthen political, economic and security ties between the U.S. and the nations of the Caribbean. The majority of TBI interventions and bulk of funding since then have supported our HIV/AIDS and trade programs. The deficiencies that became apparent after September 11 have led us to add a security dimension to the initiative. Nevertheless, because trade is also a priority, USAID is now working closely with the development assistance community, to mobilize support to respond to countries' priorities. We are conducting outreach programs that describe the benefits of free trade agreements, developing trade-related databases, implementing trade agreement commitments in such areas as customs reforms and sanitary and phytosanitary measures, providing assistance for small business development, and fostering greater civil society outreach. Meanwhile, USAID's Caribbean Regional Program is helping to strengthen Caribbean Community (CARICOM) countries' competitiveness in hemispheric and global trade, and assisting eight CARICOM countries to prepare national trade capacity building strategies as called for under the FTAA's Hemispheric Cooperation Program.

Beginning in FY 2002 USAID increased its trade capacity building activities. In Peru we have developed an Andean regional trade capacity building program to assist Andean Community countries in addressing "rules of trade" and competitiveness issues, with initial emphasis on providing technical assistance in a variety of trade disciplines including customs reforms, sanitary and phytosanitary measures, and competition policy. We also started an aggressive program to improve the regulatory and institutional framework to facilitate trade and investment and help Peru's private sector to take advantage of the Andean Trade Preferences and Drug Eradication Act (ATPDEA) and prepare for accession to the FTAA. During FY 2004, activities will focus on creating a predictable investment environment; reducing inefficiencies and transaction costs for businesses to establish and operate; and improving the regulatory framework for concessions to promote private sector investment in productive infrastructure.

An important aspect of building trade capacity is broadening the education base for a more competitive workforce. At the hemispheric level, USAID has a new "rapid response mechanism" to provide greater capacity to address technical assistance and training needs arising from trade negotiations. USAID will also support advancements in secondary education and workforce training to improve the quality of instruction, increase worker productivity, and help youths prepare to enter the workforce. For example, USAID's Training, Internships, Exchanges, and Scholarships (TIES) program in Mexico will enhance the capacity of Mexican scholars and institutions to respond to the objectives and strategies of NAFTA and the U.S./Mexico Partnership for Prosperity which together define the emerging U.S./Mexico Common Development Agenda.

USAID plans to expand assistance in the area of commercial and contract law and property rights. USAID will continue to promote rural economic diversification and competitiveness, including non-traditional agricultural exports and access to specialty coffee markets. Business development and marketing services will help small and medium farmers and rural enterprises improve competitiveness and tap new markets.

As remittances constitute a potentially large source of development finance, USAID will continue to support and implement programs that seek to "bank the unbanked" and increase the access of remittance recipients to a greater array of financial services, in addition to programs that seek to lower transaction costs.

Recognizing that economic growth must be sustainable, particularly with regard to management of natural resources, USAID is partnering with the State Department and other USG agencies on several new environmental initiatives. An example is the White Water to Blue Water Partnership Initiative (WW2BW) announced in September 2002 at the World Summit on Sustainable Development, which initially focuses on the 26 countries of the Caribbean Region. Its goal is to increase capacity in support of integrated approaches to watershed and marine ecosystem management to improve regional cooperation and communication, build partnerships to make the best use of resources, and increase government awareness. In March 2004 there will be a WW2BW "kick-off" conference in Miami designed to bring Caribbean and U.S. private and public sector stakeholders together to discuss these goals and identify areas of collaboration.

The LAC Bureau has been involved in developing and implementing the President's Initiative Against Illegal Logging, which seeks to address the negative impacts of illegal trade in timber. In Peru, there are reports that illegal loggers have developed a symbiotic relationship with resurgent terrorist groups in remote areas of Peru's tropical forests. In response, our USAID Mission in Peru is targeting more than half of its environment resources to combat illegal logging and support improved management and conservation of that country's forest resources.

Investing in People

The LAC Bureau has emphasized the Presidential priorities of health and education for our region. In health, there has been significant progress in raising vaccination coverage and in reducing or eliminating major childhood illnesses such as measles. Also, because of USAID assistance, affected countries are more willing to discuss the HIV/AIDS problem. This is particularly relevant in our region, since the Caribbean has the second highest rate of HIV/AIDS in the world. Haiti and Guyana, our two Presidential Initiative countries, have accepted expanding their fight against HIV/AIDS by initiating national programs to prevent mother to child transmission of HIV/AIDS.

While steady progress is being made to lower maternal mortality and apply proven cost-effective protocols for combating malaria, tuberculosis and other infectious diseases, rates remain unacceptably high, and new strains are increasingly resistant to treatment. As both malaria and tuberculosis are included in the Presidential Initiative for AIDS relief and the Global fund awards, we expect that resources to combat AIDS, tuberculosis and malaria will be increasing in the region. Because diseases do not respect geographic boundaries, and due to the high numbers of legal as well as illegal immigrants traveling to the United States, I believe USAID assistance to the LAC countries in health care is critical to the security and health of the United States.

The quality and relevance of primary and secondary schooling in LAC countries continue to cause concern, as the majority of youth attend weak and under-funded schools and fail to acquire basic skills in mathematics, language, and science. This is particularly true for poor and indigenous children living in rural areas. Moreover, fewer than 30% of students in the region complete secondary school, and many of those who do finish lack adequate skills to compete in the workplace, let alone in an increasingly competitive global economy. USAID education and training programs have for years improved the poor state of these public education systems through the development of innovative pilots and improved service delivery models, many of which have been carried to scale by host governments and multi-lateral development banks.

USAID has also been a leader in providing support for education policy reform through efforts such as the Partnership for Educational Revitalization in the Americans. USAID will significantly increase its focus on policy reform and government accountability in education under the new Central America and Mexico strategy, as well as in other countries where the Agency has traditionally focused primarily on service delivery. USAID will also continue enhancing the skills of teachers and administrators through the Centers of Excellence for Teacher Training, an initiative announced by President Bush in April 2001. Three sub-regional training networks established in Peru, Honduras, and Jamaica are improving the cadre of teachers in LAC countries by training up to 15,000 teachers who will serve 600,000 students.

PRIORITY COUNTRIES

Many of the democracies in the Hemisphere are fragile, and USAID works in a variety of ways in concert with other U.S. government agencies to strengthen them. I will discuss several priority countries in more detail to describe the challenges USAID faces in fostering development in support of US foreign policy.

Bolivia—To help former President Sanchez de Lozada's administration through the difficult period following protests, rioting and looting in February 2003, the State Department and USAID redirected $10 million in Economic Support Funds to support the government in a time of crisis. This assistance was used for payment of multilateral development debt and to leverage additional bilateral and multilateral contributions.

A new cycle of conflict developed in recent weeks that led to the mid-October resignation of President Sanchez de Lozada. Worker unions, coca farmers and ordinary citizens united to prevent the sale of Bolivia's underground gas deposits to the United States through a Chilean port. They are concerned that poor Bolivians will receive no benefit from the sale and demanding that some 250,000 homes be supplied with free gas connections before the export of any gas.

Illicit drug production in Bolivia and poverty continue to weaken democracy and undermine prosperity. Bolivia remains a strategic ally of the U.S. in Andean counter-drug efforts and plays a leading role in South American initiatives for democratic reform and trade liberalization. Its current economic difficulties are largely a result of external factors. Due to the success of counternarcotics efforts, coca production in Bolivia has declined an estimated 36% since 1998 at a cost of about $200 million to the Bolivian economy. The loss of this illicit income was felt most by the small-scale farmer. There is also concern that the country's economic problems, coupled with the intensive aerial eradication program in Colombia, will translate into pressure from the narcotics industry for new production in Bolivia. These concerns have heightened the importance of and the need to continue USAID's alternative development program in Bolivia.

Working in partnership with the Government of Bolivia, USAID's alternative development program is bringing the benefits of Bolivia's anti-narcotics strategy to major urban areas and market towns. As in Colombia and Peru, USAID is working to eliminate illegal and excess coca from Bolivia by: establishing sustainable, farm-level production capacity and market linkages for licit crops, and improving municipal planning capacity, social infrastructure and public health in targeted communities. Also, USAID is targeting increased resources in urban areas to provide employment and thereby diminish the pool of unemployed persons who are easily lured into the illegal drug trade. Increased emphasis will be placed on assisting small, medium and micro enterprises, and on small infrastructure projects for increasing rural competitiveness and generating employment, especially in drug prone areas. Additionally, USAID is supporting criminal justice system reforms through implementation of the new Code of Criminal Procedures as an important complement to the alternative development program.

Colombia—The scourge of narcotics threatens the social and economic fabric of Colombian society, and poses a threat to the U.S. as well. Despite the bold efforts of Colombia's strong reformist President, Alvaro Uribe, to combat narco-trafficking, lack of state presence in large portions of the country has allowed both illegal narcotics production and armed, drug-dealing terrorist organizations to continue to flourish. Drug-related spillover crimes make Ecuador's northern border vulnerable, and intensive eradication efforts by the Government of Colombia may create incentives for the narco-trafficking industry to move back into Peru and Bolivia. USAID is working in partnership with President Uribe, who is pursuing policies actively to fight narco-terrorism and expand the reach of democracy and rule of law in Colombia.

In order to provide small farmers a means to abandon illicit crop production permanently, USAID's alternative development program in Colombia seeks to increase licit income opportunities for small producers of opium poppy and coca. This program has benefited approximately 33,000 families and supported cultivation of over 30,000 hectares of licit crops such as rubber, cassava, specialty coffee, and cocoa since 2001 in regions under the influence of illicit agriculture. However, some of the coca growing areas currently are not suitable for sustainable agriculture for both agronomic and security reasons. Therefore, USAID also works with the Colombian private sector outside of the coca growing areas to increase licit income opportunities and make coca production less attractive. Infrastructure initiatives are an important component of the program. Construction of roads and bridges provides short-term employment as families make the transition to licit crops, and provide communities with physical access to markets necessary to sustain a licit economy or develop the skills and acquire funds to pursue economic alternatives. As of June 2003, USAID has helped the Government complete 410 social infrastructure projects including roads, bridges, schools, and water treatment facilities.

USAID is implementing a program to strengthen the Colombian criminal justice system, expand access to community-based legal services, promote alternative dispute resolution mechanisms, and strengthen the capacity of justice sector institutions to carry out their functions in a more timely, open, and fair manner. USAID has established 34 community-based centers for alternative dispute resolution and other legal services to increase access to justice for the urban and rural poor. Over the last seven years, the centers have handled 1.8 million cases, the majority of which are related to intra-family violence. Women represent the highest percentage of beneficiaries under the program. As a first step in facilitating Colombia's transition to a modern accusatorial system of justice, USAID has helped establish 19 oral trial courtrooms and trained 6,160 lawyers, judges, and public defenders in oral procedures designed to reduce impunity and quicken the judicial process.

USAID's transparency and accountability program seeks to harmonize accounting and internal control standards within the Government of Colombia and increase citizen awareness of available instruments to combat corruption. Last year, this program completed a public awareness anti-corruption campaign that reached six million citizens through radio, newspaper and television messages, and standardized internal control units in five government entities.

USAID is working to improve respect for human rights in Colombia and prevent human rights violations by strengthening governmental and civil society human rights institutions; protecting more than 3,000 human rights workers, community leaders, journalists, and locally elected officials under threat; and by improving Colombian government systems that respond to human rights violations. As a result, a national Early Warning System (EWS) was established and 17 regional offices opened to prevent massacres and force displacements. To date, 170 Government of Colombia responses were made to alerts issued by EWS.

Colombia has one of the largest populations of internally displaced people (IDP) in the world, about 2.5 million people, and the only IDP population in the western hemisphere. USAID has provided relief to about 1,092,000 IDPs and demobilized child soldiers, targeting aid specifically at female heads of household. Recently, the Government of Colombia has requested USAID support with the design of a demobilization and reinsertion program for ex-combatants which could be the first step toward a negotiated settlement of Colombia's prolonged civil conflict. This program will provide assistance to approximately 35,000 ex-combatants if the Government is able to sign and implement demobilization agreements with irregular armed groups that have been fighting with Government forces and each other for more than 40 years. The USG is currently assessing whether USAID should also assist the reintegration process by providing documentation, training and logistical support to ex-combatants after they have been demobilized and vetted for human rights abuses, narco-trafficking, or other criminal charges.

Haiti—I would now like to shift to the continuing challenge presented by Haiti, where poor governance and economic mismanagement has brought the country to a near standstill, and provides the impetus for continuing attempts at illegal migration to the United States, the Dominican Republic, and the Bahamas. Today, Haiti is in a state of protracted political turmoil, pervasive poverty, debilitated institutions and infrastructure, and depleted productive assets. Eighty percent of the rural population lives below the poverty line. Haiti remains by far the poorest country in the Western Hemisphere; its economic and social indicators compare unfavorably with those of many sub-Saharan African countries. Recurring droughts in some areas and heavy rains in others exacerbate the already dire conditions and place additional strains on our humanitarian relief efforts in the country. As a result of natural disasters last year, USAID provided $3.6 million in emergency food assistance.

The growing authoritarianism of President Aristide and his *Fanmi Lavalas* party frustrated USAID's efforts to bolster the Haitian judiciary and national police in the late 1990s. Consequently, we shifted our emphasis to helping civil society resist the growing authoritarianism of the Haitian government. We have added activities to strengthen political parties and the independent media. The country's direction now depends on whether the government can establish a climate for free and fair elections in 2004 and secure the participation of Haiti's opposition parties, many of which boycotted the election of President Aristide in November 2000. We also keep in close contact with the Haitian human rights community and incorporate these groups whenever possible into our activities. Last but not least, we are actively engaged with the Haitian Diaspora, seeking ways to help them foster democracy and economic growth in Haiti.

In addition to our work with civil society, USAID's programs in Haiti are designed to meet essential humanitarian needs and generate employment in a difficult economic environment. The FY 2003 AID funding was $71.5 million. The P.L. 480 Title II food program is a key element of USAID's support for humanitarian needs in Haiti, where food is distributed both through school feeding programs and principally through maternal-child health care facilities in remote areas. This approach ensures that U.S. food aid is reaching the neediest and most vulnerable Haitians, rural children under five and nursing and/or pregnant mothers. The bulk of the Title II food commodities are sold to local millers and the proceeds used to finance projects in health care (including assistance to orphans), primary education, and food production. We also put substantial resources into improving health. Haiti is one of 14 countries worldwide selected for the President's Emergency Program for AIDS Relief.

Venezuela—The political challenges facing Venezuela continue to spark protests and concern around the country. Over the past few weeks there has been movement toward a peaceful, electoral, and legal outcome to the situation in Venezuela and I would like to take a moment to update you on those events and USAID's response to them. The U.S. is a strong proponent of the recall referendum process. The constitution passed overwhelmingly in 1999 by the Venezuelan people allows for a vote to recall the president if 20 percent of the electorate sign a petition calling for a referendum. At the end of August, the Venezuela Supreme Court appointed an election board (or CNE) that will govern the process. Initial indications are that this five-member panel will mediate honestly between the Chavez government and the political opposition in navigating the rules and electoral disputes that will arise. On September 28, the CNE issued rules for the process of collecting signatures for the petition.

USAID has played an important role in promoting a peaceful resolution. Over the past year, USAID has provided over 70 grants worth over $2 million to work on Venezuela's conflict. Activities support local initiatives to find common ground on substantive issues. These often involve mayors or governors or local business and community leaders.

In addition to these efforts, USAID is working with grantees to help political parties establish a stronger role in the country and regain the trust of the electorate. We also assist organizations to conduct informal civic education workshops for leaders of neighborhood associations in poor neighborhoods in and around Caracas. USAID funds another program that monitors the status and operation of the judicial system and its operation, and works with the Venezuelan Congress to improve legislation and laws. Finally, we help organize Venezuelan civic groups to collaborate with the National Assembly in developing legislative initiatives and debate around three separate bills on municipal government, electoral procedures, and political and citizen participation.

Guatemala—As the members of this Committee are well aware, Guatemala *has recently improved its* cooperation with U.S. anti-narcotics efforts *and was re-certified by the President. Nonetheless,* corruption, organized crime and weak enforcement of the rule of law have made it difficult to promote democracy effectively. Use of death threats and kidnapping to manipulate government officials, increasing human rights violations, continued growth in crime, and concerns about citizen security all suggest that progress toward democracy has stalled in Guatemala. *Local and international observers are concerned about the level of violence in the current presidential election campaign. Despite this atmosphere,* pressure from the international community and civil society has positively influenced the government to take some significant actions that lay the groundwork for greater inclusiveness and responsiveness in Guatemala's democratic system.

USAID has been helping Guatemala's judicial sector strengthen its ability to combat corruption. USAID also helped establish an autonomous, professional public defender service throughout the country. Today, 27 USAID-assisted "justice centers" help local communities, churches, and governments access police, prosecutors, judges and public defenders to fight crime, ensure respect for human rights, and mediate disputes. Case file and information management system reforms are significantly improving efficiency while reducing the potential for corruption. The time to locate case files has dropped from several hours to less than 15 minutes, and cases are now randomly assigned to judges. Due process has improved because information on time required for various stages of court procedure is now available. The Supreme Court is using statistics on workload, productivity, case intake, and bottlenecks to improve efficiency and identify problems. A major reform of Guatemala's principal law school has been completed and a new curriculum instituted for the first year.

After several months of training and planning sponsored by USAID, eight civil society coalitions are now actively combating ethnic discrimination, promoting transparency and anticorruption, improving congressional oversight, and enhancing public security. Over the last few months, the Alliance for Transparency, a coalition of the Chamber of Commerce and two regional organizations, developed a model profile, selection criteria, and procedures to elect the new Comptroller General and focused public attention on this process for the first time. A coalition engaged in preventing crime is bringing together gang members, the media, citizens, and police in working to reduce crime in six target areas. A civil society group drafted new legislation to address domestic violence and promoted understanding and application of current laws. For the first time, local human rights organizations played an important role in the selection by the Congress of a new Human Rights Ombudsman.

POSITIVE DEVELOPMENTS

While I have discussed several issues of particular concern, I want to highlight positive developments, as well. The signing of the Inter-American Democratic Charter and the Inter-American Convention against Corruption of the Organization of American States demonstrates a commitment to good governance by LAC countries. Nicaragua is striving to curb government corruption, and other countries, such as Mexico, have also made important commitments to reduce official corruption. Recent elections in Jamaica, Brazil, Colombia, and Ecuador were all judged to be free and fair.

Ecuador continues to recover from the disastrous, twin effects of a military coup and the collapse of the economy and the banking system that befell the country in 1999. Rampant inflation and capital flight in that same year caused Ecuador to dollarize almost literally overnight, and the country experienced five changes in government in little over a year. Thanks in part to growing USAID assistance in the areas of democracy and governance and macroeconomic policy support, Ecuador has brought inflation under control and has achieved greater macro-economic stability. Moreover, USAID's assistance has enabled the GOE to obtain balance of payments assistance under a Standby Agreement with the IMF. Since the events of 1999, USAID has provided major assistance to democratic institutions, including the justice system, almost two dozen municipal governments, and the nation's electoral system. As a result of USAID's work with both governmental and non-governmental groups, Ecuador's democratic institutions have begun to improve, most notably in the areas of local government and management of electoral systems.

ALLIANCES

Private investments in Latin America, including contributions from civil society and faith-based organizations, now far exceed Official Development Assistance levels. Linking USG investments with private investments will assure a greater impact for both, as was articulated by the President at the Monterrey Conference last year. The Global Development Alliance (GDA) and the Development Credit Authority (DCA) are exciting business models where we have made the USG dollar and impact extend much farther by partnering with businesses, municipalities, universities, and philanthropic groups.

Several GDA-type partnerships are being forged in the region. For instance, due to a steep decline in coffee prices in Colombia and Ecuador, USAID partnered with *Yachana* Gourmet, the Foundation for Integrated Education and Development, the Ecuadorian Canadian Development Fund, the IDB, and *Amanecer Campesino* to combat mounting poverty. By ensuring the long-term profitability from higher prices for a premium quality cacao production, the alliance will increase the income of 3,200 families. In Brazil, we are partnering with the *Instituto de Hospitalidade*, an organization of 32 private sector, governmental and non-governmental entities, to increase employment opportunities for 600 poor youth in the tourism sector in Brazil. Another alliance, forged mainly between USAID and the local chapter of the international corruption-fighting NGO, *Transparencia por Colombia*, will oversee the distribution and refinement of a self-administered ethics course that instructs Colombian small- and medium-sized enterprises on ethical business practices. Lastly, USAID will work with Conservation International (CI), Starbucks, and the Verde-Ventures Fund to improve farmers' access to coffee niche markets and credit and develop incentives for improved conservation and socio-economic conditions. The alliance will expand upon a pre-existing CI/Starbucks alliance in Mexico by including Panama and Costa Rica.

USAID's Development Credit Authority (DCA) offers an opportunity to mobilize local capital to fund development initiatives. Through DCA, USAID provided guarantees to two Mexican microfinance institutions in the last fiscal year. The programs were designed to allow both institutions to leverage the guarantee by accessing private capital especially longer, fixed-term savings, and turning it into a significant source of lending capital. Both programs have greatly exceeded expectations, with the banks increasing total deposits by $4.8 million and $5.7 million respectively. In Guatemala, investment efforts in market towns also exceeded expectations. The Non-Traditional Exporters Guild was directly responsible for promoting $4.25 million worth of new investments in the Peace Zone and the BANCAFE Development Credit Authority mechanism leveraged an additional $4.7 million for micro-lending. In Peru, USAID has provided DCA guarantees to three rural savings and loans, allowing them to expand services in coca-growing areas. Clients will be drawn from producers who are able to meet specific market demands. Based on the DCA guarantee, USAID leveraged $12 million from the Peruvian private sector.

ENHANCING MANAGEMENT EFFICIENCY AND EFFECTIVENESS

By responding to initiatives in the President's Management Agenda, including the Strategic Management of Human Capital, USAID is maximizing the impact of foreign assistance in addressing complex development challenges. Administrator Andrew Natsios recently approved a staffing template to rationalize the allocation of staff in our overseas missions and ensure best use of personnel. Following the completion of a thorough review of management practices in several key missions in the LAC region, we have taken measures to improve efficiency by consolidating financial management and other support services in four of our LAC missions to serve sixteen country programs. In addition, we have transferred management of the ongoing regional LAC initiative to combat malaria in the Amazon to Peru in order to further improve resource effectiveness. There are many areas in which USAID is increasing efficiency; however, the many pressing priorities, new challenges, and increasing security concerns around the world are increasing the Agency's costs of doing business.

The LAC Bureau is also working creatively to improve the alignment of USAID programs with US foreign policy objectives. One of the tools to accomplish this will be an incentive-based Performance Fund to be initiated in FY 2005 that rewards good performance by countries receiving assistance. The Performance Fund will serve as an incentive to LAC missions and host countries to focus on performance, national level impact, and the achievement of measurable results.

CONCLUSION

Secretary Powell stated that no region of the world is more important to the long term prosperity and security of the United States than the region of Latin America and the Caribbean. Nowhere else do events such as political instability, terrorism, drug trafficking, and economic crises have such profound capacity to affect our national interests and the well-being of the American people. USAID programs in the region support United States foreign policy fully, promoting sustainable economic growth through support for CAFTA, FTAA, and other programs; strengthening democracy and rule of law; improving access to health care and education; and fighting the illegal trade in narcotics. At the same time as USAID's programs are effecting change across the region, we are constantly reviewing our own management and organization to maximize the impact of assistance dollars. Much remains to be done, but USAID will continue to promote a more secure, democratic, and prosperous Latin America and Caribbean region for the benefit of the American people and the international community. As President Bush has said, "this hemisphere of eight hundred million people strives for the dream of a better life, a dream of free markets and free people, in a hemisphere free from war and tyranny. That dream has sometimes been frustrated—but it must never be abandoned." There are millions of men and women in the Americas who share this vision of a free, prosperous, and democratic hemisphere. At USAID, our programs in democracy and governance, sustainable economic growth, and basic social needs are helping our friends and neighbors in the Hemisphere fulfill their aspirations.

Thank you, again Mr. Chairman for the opportunity to appear before the Subcommittee today. I welcome any questions that you and other Members of the Subcommittee may have.

Mr. BALLENGER. Thank you. Without objection, Members may submit their full statements for the record. Members will also have 5 legislative days to review and revise their comments on the record, and in addition, I have written questions I would like to submit for the record.

So without further ado, let us be polite and give Ms. Harris a chance to ask a question or two, Congresswoman.

Ms. HARRIS. Thank you, Mr. Chairman.

Welcome. It is great to see you, and thank you for all your hard work and efforts. I am sure that your appointments by President Bush send a very clear signal to Latin America of his strong intent and interest in that region as we all share.

I had a question for you, Ambassador Noriega. Specifically, we had the chance to go to Colombia a few months ago. As of March, they had gotten six Black Hawk Helicopters, in previous Administrations, I know in 2000 had gotten some 9,800 hectares of the opium, and it seems as though we have been concentrating on coca production, which is really, really important, but I did not know why we are not doing that as well for opium.

The State Department has promised that we would have 10,000 hectares of opium this year, and we are only at about 2,500, and absent political will, President Uribe certainly has it, but I think that State really needs to press much harder on that. We really have not seen that forthcoming.

Can you comment on that?

Mr. NORIEGA. Well, thank you very much for the opportunity to address that essential question.

I certainly share the deep personal commitment of you and Members of the Committee to helping Colombia address this narco-terrorism that not only attacks the institutions of that democratic government, but represents a clear threat to the United States and the health and well-being of American citizens.

We have made considerable strides as I noted on the coca side, and that is essential. On opium poppy cultivation, we have to do better. I am committed and have in—as becoming Assistant Secretary several months ago, indicated my particular interest in making sure that we do a better job on the eradication of opium poppy and the production of heroin.

To a certain extent, the helicopter resources have been distracted for other activities of particular acute need in terms of the—for example, hostage issues and other issues as the government of Colombia is prosecuting its war against these terrorist groups. But we have underscored, and I have stressed this in my meeting with my colleagues in the State Department, the absolute importance of staying after the counter-narcotics mission; that that is the way that these terrorist groups fund their activities, and we have to break that link, and that means relentless eradication.

So I can pledge to you a commitment to going back and making sure that—underscoring the importance yet again of going after the opium cultivation. I share the interest in doing that.

Ms. HARRIS. Just for the record, when we were there, I mean, it was explicitly promised by the State Department that they would get 10,000 acres. We are only at 2,500. But the data that they shared, at least when President Serrano was there, he used a lot of the folks from his country who really had a specific ax to grind. They really cared. They went after these poppy growers in the mountains, had difficulty with the cloud cover and everything else, dangerous work. But I do think that we need to continue to look at that.

And in terms of Guatemala, in your comments you said that we are going to hold Guatemala to a higher, or maybe it was Congressman Menendez, that we should hold them to a higher standard.

What really has to occur is that we must hold them to a higher standard with regard to their corruption if they are really going to stop the crossover drug trafficking.

Mr. NORIEGA. Sure. Congresswoman Harris, the last decision on certifying Guatemala was based on an assessment of how the Guatemalans had done in nine specific areas, signing a maritime agreement with the United States, seizure of illicit drugs, destruction of seized drugs that they had in storage, making progress on money laundering, asset seizure and search warrants, and precursor chemical registration, and new narcotics police regulations.

In six of these areas, the Guatemalans showed some progress. In three, some significant progress. They signed the maritime agreement. Their seizures are considerably increased, and they destroyed drugs that they had stockpiled.

When folks ask for holding them to a higher standard, as far as we are concerned we should hold them to a higher standard every year in every cycle as we make these decisions. It is in their interest, and it is certainly in ours, and it is part of our law. So I commit to you that we will definitely do that.

Ms. HARRIS. Thank you.

Mr. Franco, I had a quick question for you. On the Millennium Challenge Account, the Ranking Member, Congressman Menendez and I worked really hard on the Millennium Challenge Account, because the actual definition of how those funds would be allocated in terms of middle-income nations really was not going to provide most countries in Latin America the critical assistance that they need. There is still very large intractable pockets of poverty throughout Latin America that would change dramatically if they had the opportunity of that carrot of the Millennium Challenge Account.

I spoke with the head of the IDB today, and he shared that feeling. He said they would do their own Millennium Challenge Account so to speak.

But I want to know if you agree with that perspective, and what we can do to really offer the kind of assistance and the kind of attractive goals. Latin America has worked so hard to have democracy, and it is a difficult process, but they have not seen the economic benefits that they so desperately need, and consequently we are seeing nations really harmed by leftist political bankrupt mindsets. They are really, I think, in effect hijacking many of the indigenous people and taking them that way, and so you are not seeing democracy. You are seeing 20,000 govern, you know, the country.

And I think that the types of assistance the Millennium Challenge Accounts offer in terms of investing in people with health care and education, or the rule of law, making sure that the corruption has a low factor, and then certainly the economic reforms are absolutely vital, and Latin America tends to be very, very responsive to those kind of grants.

Mr. FRANCO. Yes, thank you very much for the question, Congresswoman.

In response, and I have been involved in some of these discussions, and as you know all of this, there is not a Millennium Challenge Account yet established, and money yet needs to be appropriated. In fact, the program needs to be authorized.

But the President has articulated a number of standards, and among them income, people have honed in their objective standards, income, per capita income is one of them, and that would, for example, include—exclude immediately from MCA qualifications as we know them to be large countries such as Brazil and Mexico, which have very large populations that are very impoverished people. Northeast Brazil, for example, 53 million people live between a dollar and two dollars a day.

Yet based on the criteria that we have today it would be very difficult to envision how Brazil would qualify for MCA, or a country such as Mexico.

But if I can answer it two ways. The President's vision for MCA is to—as you correctly stated—to encourage countries to, number one and foremost, attack corruption; and then secondly, invest in their people, particularly on health and education.

And the idea of the MCA is to reward those countries on just that basis, and which is very important as the road to prosperity, which we all, I think, share.

The problem is in our region, and you are right, there is some income distributions, there is some skewed data that makes it difficult to address poverty in certain parts of the region. Our hope, however, is that—and I know that Chairman Ballenger, we were in Brazil together, the countries that have these large pockets, we want to help poor countries, and I think the MCA, as the President has defined it, will do that, because they are the lower income countries that are investing in people that really will get the lion's share of the MCA.

The problems of Mexicos and Brazils and larger countries it is our hope that working with countries that have the resources, such as in the case of Brazil, a country that has embarked upon a fomazado program to attack poverty, that the principles of the MCA in working with our other bilateral programs we can encourage investments in larger societies that have more resources to meet the President's MCA goals from within.

In other words, we have bilateral programs. MCA, as you know, is not to supplant or replace our current foreign assistance programs, but it is designed to help those poorest, poorest countries that are making the necessary reforms. It is our hope that the ones that still have large pockets but have resources can be encouraged with other bilateral programs which we have to make investments in their people since they have more resources to do so.

Mr. BALLENGER. Thank you. Let me see if I can make this thing work.

Congressman Delahunt. I am not penalizing anybody. I just wanted to make sure I could make this work.

Mr. DELAHUNT. Good job, Mr. Chairman. [Laughter.]

Welcome to both of you. I concur with, let me associate myself with the remarks of the Ranking Member, at least most of them.

Mr. NORIEGA. He said some nice things about me. Is that the part that you——

Mr. DELAHUNT. That is the part I wanted——[Laughter.]

Mr. NORIEGA. It did not last very long. He was on a roll——

Mr. DELAHUNT. No. Seriously, I think that your advent as a permanent secretary is important, and I have great respect for Mr. Franco, as I do for you, Mr. Secretary.

But at the same time I think as we look at the landscape of Latin America, you know, honesty compels us to really conclude that we are in a crisis. One can list the countries. I think it was you, Roger, who mentioned Cuba, Venezuela, and Haiti. Paraguay has been a single-party state for how many years now? For decades. Certainly not an example of a vibrant, healthy democracy. We had great hopes in Peru in the aftermath of Fugimori. There clearly is great social tension there. The last time I noticed the approval ratings for President Toledo were in the single digits. We have a real crisis here.

And I welcome your remarks, Secretary Noriega. I read your statement before your confirmation hearing. There is much in there that I agree with. I think that we are getting on the same page.

But the problem that I really have is that we are trying to do this on the cheap. It is a question of the magnitude of the commitment. One can list the nations in Latin America that are in serious trouble. It is a region in which I think we all share a profound concern and cannot be limited to any single country.

You talked briefly about Brazil. It is my understanding that, you know, violent criminal syndicates have all but taken over the cities in Brazil. In Argentina, the middle class has disappeared.

I believe this is the last chance. If we are going to seriously respect our own rhetoric, we have got to step up. We have to start to think large. We are sending a billion dollars a month to Afghanistan, and I support that. But when one reviews the aggregate in terms of assistance to Latin America, absent Plan Colombia, it is below a billion dollars. It just is not going to happen.

You can come here and testify, you are individuals of good will, but you have got to become advocates within the Administration in terms of stressing the need to deliver, deliver.

Adolfo, you just mentioned when the Millennium Challenge Account is finally authorized, but we are not even there yet. The Ranking Member, Mr. Menendez, and I have been working on this concept with the Chairman for a center for strengthening of democratic institutions, as well as his idea and concept of a social and economic investment fund. These are begging for action. We need to work together with you to make sure it happens quickly because if it does not, Bolivia is just the beginning. It is just the beginning. And we will all regret the fact that we have not moved more expeditiously.

Let me just digress for 1 minute and mention Guatemala, as others have here already. Recently, I co-chaired a caucus on human rights, and it had to do with the issue of Guatemala, and the possibility of an individual who many suggest was implicated in a serious way in the genocide that occurred in Guatemala during the 1980s. I am speaking of Mr. Rios Montt. There was testimony from the Administration that they were not happy with the situation.

I am currently forming in my own mind a sense of Congress resolution, or possibly a letter. I want to consult with the Chairman and Mr. Menendez and other Members of the Committee. The possibility of Mr. Rios Montt, if these allegations are true, becoming the next President of Guatemala has got to be totally unacceptable.

I would hope that the Administration would go back and review the evidence that is outstanding against Mr. Rios Montt, the charges that are currently posited in various international tribunals, and encourage through its influence that those charges be pursued or be prosecuted, and let the truth come out, because for the United States to find itself in a position to deal with an individual who is guilty of crimes against humanity that border on the same magnitude of Saddam Hussein is absolutely unacceptable.

If you have any comment, I would welcome to hear it.

Mr. BALLENGER. Go ahead. The red light went on before he asked his first question.

Mr. NORIEGA. I appreciate the opportunity. Let me do the Guatemala reference first, and then I want to talk about several of the other points, if you do not mind.

We are in agreement, Congressman Delahunt, of the grave implications of the possible election of Rios Montt as President of Guatemala. We have made known our views on that subject, and what we can do to deal with the possible election, or that is to say how we would move as part of the international community to hold him accountable for these alleged crimes.

I would want to set it apart from this electoral environment.

Mr. DELAHUNT. Absolutely.

Mr. NORIEGA. Because, quite frankly, we have to calculate that it may—that U.S. comments on this subject might actually backfire and generate some national support for him, and we would not want to be accused of doing that either.

Incidently, if I can say parenthetically, I think that on other cases in other elections, I think we need to be careful generally in how we deal with these. There have been recent examples where we have been pretty heavy-handed, quite frankly, in letting our views be known. I would think it is much better for us to, particularly in an electoral environment, be careful about that sort of thing.

Mr. DELAHUNT. I welcome that caveat.

Mr. NORIEGA. I know you were addressing Paraguay parenthetically in this, and not necessarily with particular purpose, but let me comment on that briefly.

You have a new President of Paraguay, Nicanor Duarte Frutos, who is absolutely committed to cleaning up the corruption in his country. He has named an economic minister and finance minister that are not part of his party, or independent persons, business people who will come into the government to serve the government and to clean up what is widely regarded as rampant corruption. Corruption being theft from the people.

And Paraguay's economic woes are fueled in part by that as well as an economic downturn. The reason I mention that is he has in just a matter of 2 months or so increased tax revenues to the state by 35 percent. We asked him how did you do this. He said,

> "I fired a few people who were stealing all the money. I am holding people accountable that are not paying their taxes, and I am firing the people who stole the tax revenues that were paid."

It is remarkable then how these measures taken by a leader himself, by government himself when they hold themselves accountable to taking these steps, what remarkable difference that they can make.

There also was a statement about the impact of corruption which undermines any sort of economic development efforts, drives away investment. There is a classic crisis of expectations in the Americas. Countries and peoples, populations that have done the right things, done what the international community asked of them, and now they see very few results, and part of it is the economic downturn in the late nineties. After a period of growth, unemployment is up, inflation is up, growth is flat or down, and we have not turned that around. We have to make a concerted effort to do this.

We may be accused of having trade and investment high up on our agenda, but there is a reason for that. I gave you one illustration, that the income from trade, the income from what we import from these countries is 600 times our development, and where we—where we are putting our development assistance is those countries that need it most. It may be regarded as a small sum or relatively small sum, under a billion dollars, but we are putting it in countries that are least able to help themselves and where the needs are most acute. We are not going to spend a lot of money in development assistance in Argentina and Brazil. These are relatively well-off countries. And to the extent that there are impoverished sectors of those economies, it is the responsibility of the state to use its own resources, not U.S. tax dollars to turn that around, and to put the right policies in place to extend opportunity to those parts, and develop those parts of their own country, and to use their credit worthiness to attract investment and trade, and international financial institution resources to do that for themselves.

That is what I want to underscore. So many of the obstacles to economic progress, economic growth can be moved by the levers that are in the hands of these people themselves, the governments themselves. We can help them. We do help them. We do have leadership on this. We do have engagement on trade and the rule of law and democracy. So we do contribute that way. We do have MCA on the way to make significant increases in our assistance, but it is what countries have to do for themselves in putting the right policies in place to turning their economies around, and I have a couple of illustrations on that point.

Mr. BALLENGER. Let me step in, if I may.

Adolfo, I need to ask a question of you. Many Nicaraguans on the side of the most acute poverty in that country, are where the presence of the state is tenuous at best. Is USAID prepared to provide sustained support for the OAS's successful effort in this part of Nicaragua to help rural campasinos and organizations such as the Peace and Justice Commission?

Mr. FRANCO. Yes, Mr. Chairman. The short answer to that is yes, and I will just give you an illustration.

We are actually helping the OAS commissions at the current time to the tune of $1.25 million, and I think this is extremely important work which we would like to expand and have a longer term commitment.

This has also been a priority of the Bolanos administration. It is an area—speaking of the poverty, Nicaragua is a very poor country, but you are talking about the poorest part of a very poor country where the state presence is also very critical.

So it is also, in terms of longer term potential for development and markets, an area in which I think the Bolanos administration has correctly identified as it has great potential. So we will be working to—very happy to report to the Committee we are working the commissions, and we will continue to do so in the future.

I will be in Nicaragua next week, and this is a subject that I will discuss with the mission, with the Embassy, and report back to you on.

If I could just very briefly just add just a couple of comments to Mr. Delahunt's and Secretary Noriega's comments. I fully concur with what the Assistant Secretary has outlined. I will say on the Guatemala front, in addition to the diplomatic efforts and other communications that the Secretary and others, I know Ambassador Hamilton conveyed to the government of Guatemala, USAID is working to ensure that there are free and fair elections in Guatemala.

We are investing United States Government resources, $2.5 million in that country, and USAID is providing $750,000 for municipal level education, voter registration. Fortunately, the tribunal, the supreme tribunal, electoral tribunal that works in the country is good. It is a good partner. So we are doing everything possible on the electoral front to assure that the election is not stolen, so we are very much engaged in that effort.

Just by coincidence, just on President Frutos and Paraguay, I know it is just an illustration, but I did meet with the development ministry last week, and I will be in Paraguay in early November, just to underscore what Secretary Noriega has said. I think there is a dramatic change in that country, I see a change, a commitment to address corruption. That is at the pillar or core of our programs at USAID.

One of the things the minister told me, we are not talking about a lot of money here. He said we are talking about political commitment and will. Will you support us? Will you continue to support us as we present—I think Secretary Noriega was referring to the levers at the World Bank and at the IDB—will you support us in our efforts if we show results? And the answer to that is yes.

So I wanted to use those as illustrations, but I fully concur that with our money we can leverage additional resources from the international community.

Mr. BALLENGER. Let me throw one—my time hasn't ended yet. Last week or a week before last President Uribe was here.

Mr. MENENDEZ. Take all the time you want, Mr. Chairman. [Laughter.]

Mr. BALLENGER. And he was here and he brought up, somebody brought up the question of some of the prisoners that had been captured there, one of them being Carlos Castania. Well, why in the world was he not being indicted and put in jail and so forth and so on?

President Uribe came up with what—since I have been involved in El Salvador and in Nicaragua—both of those countries when the war stopped in El Salvador, everybody was forgiven. Even if they had been murdering 25–30 people, they were forgiven. Same thing held true when Mrs. Chamorro took over Nicaragua, and she just said, look, we have got to forgive and reconcile all our differences, and basically both those two countries worked.

President Uribe now has, I know, at least 2,500 of the FARC, ELN and AUC, have all decided to quit, and he came up with this thing of educating these people instead of putting them in prison, and instead of indicting them for murder or anything like that.

I am helping out a little bit myself there, but have they asked us for our assistance? To my way of thinking, it is the most natural thing in the world to get peace in Colombia.

Mr. FRANCO. Well, we are looking at that. You mentioned El Salvador. As I recall, "the reinsertion" is what we called it. I know you, Mr. Chairman, have had a lot of experience in Central America, and El Salvador and Nicaragua as well. We are looking into it and we are exploring it: Our mission in Columbia is doing assessments and it is reviewing this very carefully.

The Colombians have not come to us specifically with a program, but we are engaged with them as to what the program would entail in terms of providing employment, educational opportunities, and other things to make former combatants productive members of society.

It is absolutely essential when we get to the appropriate time to have—I hope—a comprehensive program to give people who were ex-combatants that opportunity. That was one of the reasons we had a spike up, as you might all recall, in crime for some period of time in El Salvador, which we have brought under control since that time.

But one of the things we—we are not waiting for, USAID, is for the day when the documents are signed. We see that coming on the horizon. We have had some positive indicates that there is movement in that direction, and we are making all the preparations for it.

I will say this since resources are on everybody's mind. This was, as you know, in El Salvador, Mr. Chairman, a very expensive proposition, something that with the current resources we have at USAID, we would not be able to handle. It is an expensive, but absolutely necessary program.

Mr. BALLENGER. To save you a little bit of money, there are two container loads of school furniture going through with United States Southern Command (SOUTHCOM) this week, just happen to be coming from North Carolina.

Mr. FRANCO. We will work with you on that. I think I am seeing General Hill next week.

Mr. BALLENGER. Mr. Menendez.

Mr. MENENDEZ. Thank you, Mr, Chairman, and I want to thank the gentlelady from Florida for her continuing interest in trying to find a way in the hemisphere to be more helpful than what MCA promises. I appreciate her continuing interest. After a decade, I am more than exasperated here of sitting on this Committee and listening to multiple Administrations give me the same line.

The reality is, is that, Mr. Secretary, when you say in your testimony on page 7, "We will encourage countries to invest in people so that they can claim their fair share of economic opportunity and improve their quality of life," and go on to the President referring to it as "prosperity with a purpose." You have, Mr. Franco, a $839 million total budget for Latin America, which you spent in excess of a couple of hundred million between just Colombia and Haiti. You cannot fulfill those goals. That is the simple reality of it.

We can come here and we can sugarcoat it and we can do whatever we want. You have $839 million, spent a couple of hundred million between just Colombia and Haiti, and the rest of the hemisphere is left with the balance. I understand your vision. You describe the President's vision for MCA.

Unfortunately, I would love to tell the President your vision for MCA is not being realized, at least for Latin America, in the context of its present iteration.

So we are not going to get that vision unless it is dramatically changed. There were opportunities for the Administration to come forth and say that it is important for Latin America to have a greater participation in MCA, and you all chose not to do it for whatever the reason.

So the bottom line is is that we are not going to get to where you want to be, where I will subscribe all the best purposes for where you want to be, so long as we are locked into this effort. And so, you know, I do not expect you to answer, even in agreement with me, because that would put the Administration in a position of saying, yes, we agree. But the reality is that we must have a development fund that increases our efforts. I am not even talking about those countries that have resources. I am talking about a whole host of countries. You know that we want to stop illegal immigration, and you want to stop—give people alternatives to narcotics. You want to give people alternatives to be able to develop a greater middle class market so that more American goods and services could be used. You want to stop some of the trends that we see in health issues that are coming along the border and into the United States. We have an enormous interest. And I do not even want to know how many billions we have spent in Central America under President Reagan to promote democracy.

And now we spend less than a couple hundred million dollars in the entire hemisphere for development work. So when it is time to go to use force, we are willing to go to unlimited amounts of money. When it is time to take the seeds of democracy that we sow and have them grow into a fertile harvest, we do not take that opportunity.

I hope that we can move in a different direction in this effort than simply taking the hard line, stonewall, we can do with what we have got.

And yes, 600 times the income, but you are just growing the disparity. You are just growing the disparity, and therefore you continue to promote, I think, unwittingly the seeds of discontent in the hemisphere.

Yes, that trade is important, but trade unmatched with any development help is simply not going to put us where we need to be. So I just make that statement.

Now, I have a few quick questions, and Mr. Secretary, if you would work with me to try to get answers a quickly as possible before that light goes out.

Number one is, one of the benefits of being here after awhile you get some institutional history. You were one of those individuals in your former position that helped us draft Helms-Burton. A task force after 3 years? A task force after 3 years? Waiving—why do we waive title 5? We always excoriated the previous Administration for doing it. Why do we not enforce title 4? Why do we continue to repatriate Cubans who are living, who are seeking to be free from tyranny on the high seas and come to the United States, over 1,000 of them? Where is the difference in the policy?

Mr. NORIEGA. Mr. Menendez, let me just address that in a fulsome way if I could. President Bush has stated that he will not make unilateral concessions to Castro.

Mr. MENENDEZ. I heard you say that in your statement.

Mr. NORIEGA. I know, I understand. We never heard President Clinton say that.

Mr. MENENDEZ. Why do we continue to waive title 5?

Mr. NORIEGA. My point is, Mr. Menendez, is we never heard President Clinton say that, and from my experience I remember begging——

Mr. MENENDEZ. Why do we continue to waive title 5?

Mr. NORIEGA. Am I allowed to comment?

Mr. MENENDEZ. I asked you three specific questions. Title 5, title 4, wet foot/dry foot policy.

Mr. NORIEGA. You also asked a fourth question which I prefer to answer first, what is the difference.

I remember begging Administration representatives under the previous Administration to at least help us stop—staunch the undermining of the U.S. pressure on Castro, and we got no support, not the slightest bit of support from the previous Administration.

President Bush has said there will be no unilateral concessions to the regime, and that we will reserve our support—making any changes in our policy, that we will not change the embargo until it is to deepen economic and political change in Cuba that will wipe away vestiges of the Castro regime. We never got that from the Clinton Administration.

Seven years ago when Helms-Burton was signed, the number of joint ventures that were being signed by the Castro regime were in the dozens every month. Now, I think there were maybe 50 last year.

The Helms-Burton law, in my judgment, has served the purpose of signaling the people that they cannot do business as usual and abusing confiscated property, confiscated from U.S. nationals; that the tool of title 3, we have investigations underway with respect to several different properties, and I can get you some, brief you on——

Mr. MENENDEZ. Not one action in 3 years?

Mr. NORIEGA. There has not been, no.

Mr. MENENDEZ. Why do we continue to waive title 5?

Mr. NORIEGA. I think you are referring to title 3.

Mr. MENENDEZ. The ability for U.S. companies to——

Mr. NORIEGA. It is title 3.

Mr. MENENDEZ. Title 3.

Mr. NORIEGA. We did not get to five. Maybe there was another idea out there. But title 3 was—the last waiver that we made was based on increasing consensus in the world that Castro had to—was not going to change; that he was—the crackdown on dissidents underscored for the first time in a very clear way to the international community, the Europeans in particular, and even some in Latin America, that there had to be some meaningful steps to encourage Castro to provide some kind of political freedom and economic freedom, and free the dissidents that were jailed in the springtime.

Our decision on title 3, and we can rescind it and make change any time the President chooses to do so, is based on keeping up multilateral international pressure and not repolarizing the issue so that the issue becomes how is the U.S. Government treating property that was stolen from U.S. nationals.

Mr. MENENDEZ. Mr. Secretary, with all due respect, with all due respect, President Clinton was excoriated by my colleagues on this Committee, by colleagues on the Full Committee, and by others because he waived title 3, the right to sue, because he did not enforce title 4 vigorously, they had one prosecution in 3 years.

You have waived title 3 six times already, or five times already. You have continued to pursue the wet foot/dry foot policy. The reality is there is no difference except rhetoric between this Administration and the previous Administration. Now, rhetoric is great, but there is no difference whatsoever.

Now, Mr. Chairman, I have a series of other questions and I see my time has expired, so I hope there will be a second round since we very rarely have a hearing, and very rarely have the Secretary. I have a series of other questions, but in deference to my colleagues I will hold the rest of them.

Mr. BALLENGER. Congressman Payne, it is your turn to take a shot.

Mr. PAYNE. Well, I think that it is certainly pretty clear that there is dissatisfaction on this side of the table anyway about what is going on. I also am baffled at the lack of importance attached to our Latin American, Central and South American and Caribbean. They call it the third gateway, the Caribbean, for example, and as Mr. Menendez very clearly pointed out, the amount of development assistance and other kinds of aid is just paltry compared to the needs.

Poverty is increasing. Governance is getting worse. The whole question of unsettled countries are increasing, and it is very serious because it has a lot of impacts, first of all, it is part of the Americas, and as a young fellow I remember when President Kennedy had the whole new move to bring the Americas together, and I have not seen very much beef put on the policies.

One, I wonder, is there any possibility that a strengthening of the OAS or a move to make sort of more of a union as they have tried in NAFTA with the UA and Europe you see with the Europe being a common community? Do you think that there would be any positive moves if somehow Latin America could have a strong organization that may be able to be able to advocate for themselves?

Mr. NORIEGA. Well, Congressman Payne, the OAS does play an important role, and it should be strengthened. It is strengthened in part by our engagement in the organization, and taking it seriously, and looking for multilateral solutions, and using it as an instrument.

Just very briefly a couple of examples where we have used it. On the drug fight, we have an Inter-American Commission on Drug Abuse Control, which brings all of the countries together around one table to negotiate standards, negotiate measures that would have to be taken by each of these countries to apply within their own national territory to fight drugs.

We have a multilateral evaluation mechanism where experts grade the countries on how they do and recommend how they could do better from year to year, and we use that commission as a means of providing technical assistance so countries can do a better job of meeting their commitments. So it is a very positive model where you have multilateral model, expert-driven evaluation, and then providing technical support to help countries to live up to their commitments.

We are doing the same thing on the terrorism front. We just started an Inter-American Committee on Education, which could potentially take a look at how do countries spend their education dollars, because no matter how big our aid program is, it is going to be dwarfed by what a national government is spending in its own territory and in its own public schools.

So can we find a way to have the most effective—what are the best educational policies, what is the best investment for education dollars in terms of maybe it is better to spend it in secondary school rather than paying for 12 years of college, and put the dollars into secondary, which is a broader-based investment.

My vision would be to use this multilateral organization to put those kinds of policies in place in the social areas, and to provide some discrete inputs on development strategies. The OAS advises countries on the trade competitiveness and how they can be more competitive as we move toward a more Free Trade Areas in the Americas, for example.

I think multilateralism does work in the Americas because of our shared values, and because of our shared objectives, and we should definitely stress it.

I think it is important that our trade policy is pursued in a multilateral way through the Free Trade Areas in the Americas, because we understand that, as attractive as bilateral agreements are, multilateral agreements are just as important, if not more important, because the trade among these countries, not just with the United States, is where their real economic potential can be, and so that is why we pursue the trade agenda in a multilateral way through the Free Trade Area of the Americas and why that is important.

So I could go on at some length about the effectiveness of these institutions. They require our participating and our putting some resources behind them.

Mr. PAYNE. That is fine. I guess I will not even ask the other questions, but I had thought, just thinking in terms of how the recent outrage in Cancun about agricultural subsidies in the developed world, you know, it is about a billion dollars a week around the world that is spent between EU, United States and Japan, and it is going to make it hard for indigenous farmers to ever be able to compete, but I will let that—since the red light is on, I will yield back. I guess I am out of time, it is frustrating.

Are you sure that clock is not——

Mr. BALLENGER. I do not think so.

Mr. PAYNE. Okay, well, a long count with the dentist——

Mr. BALLENGER. Like I say, everybody spoke past the length of the clock so it did not bother me.

Mr. PAYNE. Okay.

Mr. BALLENGER. You did too, so it did not make any difference. Congressman Weller.

Mr. WELLER. Thank you, Mr. Chairman. I apologize for being delayed in arriving. Mr. Secretary, Mr. Administrator, good to see you, and I appreciate the opportunity to be here.

I realize this panel here you have been working with them for some time, and again I apologize for the delay, but you know, this week there is important elections in Colombia, and we have seen the FARC and the other left-wing guerrillas who have been funded through narcotics trafficking targeting elected officials, intimidating elected officials, intimidating candidates, committing assassinations against those who hold public office in Colombia.

And I was just wondering, can you give us a report, just kind of tell us what the status is, what the current situation is there, and how you expect to see this progress through the elections later this week?

Mr. NORIEGA. I will ask Adolfo Franco to talk about the program we have to provide security for candidates, which is an important program. And it is true that these narco-terrorist gangs are desperate to undermine the democratic process, and they have been pursued vigorously by the Uribe administration, and before them by the Pastrana administration, and they are under a lot of pressure. They are absolutely committed to intimidating people who want to invest in the future and participate in a democratic process and serve their country, serve their communities, to intimidate them out of the process and undermine the system of accountable government and democratic values, and it shows us their desperation.

It is not new. It is what the guerrillas have done in Colombia before, and for that matter, in El Salvador and elsewhere in the past as a way of weakening democratic institutions.

I will let Adolfo talk a little bit about how we are responding to this.

Mr. FRANCO. Thank you, Congressman Weller.

Our program in Colombia has three major components. One is alternative development, another is assistance to displaced people, and the third is the Rule of Law and Justice Program.

Within that program, we do two things that are a little bit unusual for a development agency, but they reflect the reality as you know, Congressman Weller, very well of Colombia. They have to do with a protection system to protect mayors and others that have the courage to participate in Colombia's democratic system.

As part of that effort to help his democratic security agenda, we provide protection to mayors and others that are in the limelight. We have a protection system that goes beyond just candidates, but also supports in varying degrees, working with the Colombian Ministry of the Interior, journalists, union leaders, anyone who is participating in the political process that is either targeted or receives a credible threat against their lives or their families. We provide protection that varies from the type of protection that you might envision, such as guards, to really the extreme of having support to leave the country based on the work that we do with the Minister of the Interior.

The other is an early warning system that we support, which is the equivalent—I do not want to give it short shrift here—of a 911, which is having communities and others alert a national system so that appropriate central government authorities can be deployed to a specific area that is going to be targeted by the FARC or terrorists because of a lack of state presence or insufficient local authorities in affected areas. This is a way for central authority to respond.

Mr. NORIEGA. And complementing that just very briefly, the Colombian government itself has a very conscious policy and strategy of putting security forces, military and police, into the communities to impose the rule of law, put the presence of the state out in front. President Uribe has targeted about 170 communities, he is in about 150 of them now.

Mr. FRANCO. That is part of his democratic security agenda, which is bring in the state presence, and really retaking—retaking Colombia back community by community, which we fully support.

Mr. WELLER. Well, I certainly believe that is an important investment for our government. There is no more important common value that we share with Latin America than our belief in democracy and freedom, and I believe Colombia, and please correct me if I am incorrect, is the oldest longstanding democracy in all of South America, so that work is extremely important.

Can you share with us essentially what the casualty loss has been with this direct attack by the FARC and others on these elected officials?

It is my understanding, the figures I have seen give up to 25 local officials have been assassinated by the FARC and their allies?

Mr. NORIEGA. That sounds right. I remember looking at this number late last week or maybe even over the weekend, and that seems about right, and people resigning their candidacies too, and that is another thing, and it is a very concerted campaign of the guerrillas to force people out. It is remarkable, frankly, that so many do serve in spite of the fact that they are literally under fire.

Mr. WELLER. Thank you. Thank you, Mr. Chairman.

Again, I apologize for being late.

Mr. BALLENGER. That is all right. No problem. And let me apologize to Dr. Pastor. I was going to cut it off, but Congressman Weller said he had a couple of short questions, and I think we got the answer to the questions. If we were all on the Appropriations Committee like Mr. Weller, then we would not have any problems at all. We would give you everything you all need to solve that problem, but go ahead Mr. Menendez.

Mr. MENENDEZ. Thank you, Mr. Chairman. Mr. Chairman, if we have more hearings, then they can be shorter in breadth. But when we do not, we have to take advantage of the opportunities we can.

Mr. Secretary, you talk about Mexico being an important partner. Yet when they did not side with us on our issue with Iraq, war with Iraq, we sort of froze them out. My question is, when are we going to see a migration agreement with Mexico, which is in our national interest and in our national security interest?

Mr. NORIEGA. Well, let me underscore, and I will get to the migration question in just 2 seconds, let me——

Mr. MENENDEZ. If you eat up my time, I really need to to focus on my question——

Mr. NORIEGA. Okay, let me just say——

Mr. MENENDEZ [continuing]. Which is, when are we going to get a migration agreement with Mexico? Are we going to get a migration agreement?

Mr. NORIEGA. Mr. Menendez, the migration issue is a matter of great importance, not just in our relations with Mexico, but to our own security here as you have alluded to, the importance of having a reliable system of determining who is in the United States and give them reliable identification. It is something we need to address in a global way. It is something that the Administration has focused considerable attention on. It has nothing to do really with any tension we have had with the Mexican government.

We note with some interest the new initiatives in Congress that signal a sense of receptiveness in the Congress where these immigration laws would have to be made. And while I am not in a position to, of course, announce any new initiatives on it, let me just say that it is something that is very much front and center in the Administration's agenda of considering possible initiatives on that front.

Mr. MENENDEZ. When the President had President Fox on the ranch, migration was at the top of that. It is certainly on the top of President Fox's agenda as well. And my concern is that if you are going to wait for Congress, we need the Administration, as it has when it wants to, to say that we believe a migration accord is important and necessary and in our mutual interest, and that has not been forthcoming. So I urge the Administration to do.

And you heard my opening statement as it relates to some of the CAFTA countries that I am concerned about. Are you aware of some of the facts that I have raised about the Dominican Republic?

Mr. NORIEGA. Yes, sir, absolutely.

Mr. MENENDEZ. And what are we doing about it?

Mr. NORIEGA. Well——

Mr. MENENDEZ. What do we know about it?

Mr. NORIEGA. The Dominican government is dealing with what is extraordinary broad crisis of corruption where a particular family had a very vast network of corruption that reaches into basically every facet of Dominican life, having people on the payroll and is part of the corrupt network of doing his business.

To its credit, the Dominican government has stepped in to at least indemnify people who had money in accounts.

Mr. MENENDEZ. By his own credit card.

Mr. NORIEGA. That I am not familiar with.

Mr. MENENDEZ. I would urge you to review——

Mr. NORIEGA. Sure, I will take a look at that.

Mr. MENENDEZ [continuing]. It and get back to the Committee. There are millions of dollars charged to a credit card issued to the government.

Mr. NORIEGA. Well, I will be glad to take a look at that and let you know about that.

Mr. MENENDEZ. Are you familiar with the issue of buying sophisticated equipment that would not have been sold by the Israeli government outside of the security, then the Dominican government then had that resold to the——

Mr. NORIEGA. No, I am not.

Mr. MENENDEZ. I would urge you to look at that——

Mr. NORIEGA. I will do that.

Mr. MENENDEZ [continuing]. And report back to the Committee.

I have a series of other questions, Mr. Chairman. I am going to submit them for the record, but I am going to at each hearing that we have, if I do not get an answer to them, because it takes 6 months to get an answer generally speaking from the department, I am not saying from this gentleman, if it takes 6 months to get an answer, then it is if no value——

Mr. NORIEGA. Yes.

Mr. MENENDEZ [continuing]. To ask a question in writing. So each and every time, whether on the Floor if I have to go on the

Floor, or in other Committee hearings unrelated, I am going to raise the questions if it is not in a reasonable timely answer as to what is the use of submitting questions if you cannot get a timely answer, and I thank you.

Mr. BALLENGER. If I may offer a comment to this migration situation. President Fox was here and it just so happened that as a Senior Member on the Committee, I was able to meet with him. He got up and made a speech that we are going to act like the Rio Grande is not there, and everybody is going to go back and forth, and it is going to be wonderful, peace and quiet. Everybody is going to move back and forth.

And as I sat there, I had a chance to ask the question as you did, and I said,

> "Well, President Fox, let me pose to you a question. I have a little two-bit operation down in North Carolina, manufacturing plant, and in it I have two Salvadorans, two Costa Ricans, seven Guatemalans, and five Mexicans. Now, you want me to pass a bill to take care of the five Mexicans. What do I do with the rest of the people?"

And he said, "You have a very difficult problem."

So let me just thank both of you fellows for dealing with us in a very intelligent way, and I want to thank you for participating. Yes, sir, fire away.

Mr. NORIEGA. May I say just—I appreciate the comments that have been made, particularly about the resources issues, and I look forward to working with the Subcommittee and Members on both sides of the aisle on that, and I will provide any answers. I will try to get them up here as quickly as I possibly can. I do not know how long it takes to get things after I clear them, but we will do our darndest to get them up here rather quickly.

Thank you very much.

Mr. BALLENGER. Thank you both.

Now, Mr. Pastor, Dr. Pastor, excuse me. Robert Pastor has been the Vice President of International Affairs and a Professor of International Relations at American University since September 2000.

Dr. Pastor previously was a Professor at Emory University, and Director of the Carter Center's Latin American and Caribbean Program. Dr. Pastor was the Director of Latin American Affairs on the National Security Council during the Carter Administration from 1977 to 1981.

Welcome, Dr. Pastor. Could you please proceed by summarizing your opening statements? Without objection, we will submit the full statement for the record.

STATEMENT OF ROBERT A. PASTOR, VICE PRESIDENT OF INTERNATIONAL AFFAIRS, AMERICAN UNIVERSITY

Mr. PASTOR. Thank you very much, Mr. Chairman, Congressmen Menendez, Congressman Delahunt, Congressman Weller. I commend the Committee for focusing on our neighbors at a time when the Administration and most of our country's attention is elsewhere. I especially commend you for your persistence, interest, and patience in remaining here for this whole hearing.

When President Bush was elected, Latin American expectations were quite high. He was the only of the two candidates to give a special speech just to Latin America, in which he promised that Latin America would, "not be an afterthought;" that it would be central to his policy. He pledged to President Fox and to Prime Minister Chretien that our relations with our two closest neighbors would be of the greatest importance to him.

He has not delivered on those promises, and indeed since he came to office Latin America's economy has worsened significantly, and Secretary Powell himself said at the swearing-in ceremony for Roger Noriega that Latin America was suffering from "a level of dissatisfaction with the quality of democracy and the results of economic reform."

I think the word "dissatisfaction" is an understatement. The progressive President of Bolivia was just thrown out of office by a mob. His neighbors in the Andes are on the precipice of either economic chaos or political instability. The engine of South America, Brazil, is stalled. The second great economic power in South America, Argentina, is in default and has lost a quarter of its GDP in the last 2 years.

And our relations with our two closest neighbors, partly as a result of divergence of perspectives on Iraq, have sunk to a level that they had not seen for decades.

So the question really is, what do we do? We have a full agenda. The most striking feature of President Bush's policy to our neighbors is simply that there is little of it, and while the rhetoric seemed quite attractive, it seems inconsistent with their deeds, or there is very little follow up, as you have just found in the inadequate answers to your own questions.

Secretary Powell should be credited for signing the Inter-American Democratic Charter. But what does that mean when there are others in the Administration who supported the coup in Venezuela, who were chastised by the rest of Latin America for it? What does support for the democratic charter mean when the Administration's Ambassadors in Bolivia and in El Salvador take sides in a presidential election despite the fact that there is a history in which the United States did not support the democratic process unless that process yielded a result to our favor?

I acknowledge the comment by Assistant Secretary Noriega a little while ago that, in effect, the Administration had been heavy-handed in its comments on elections in Latin America, and that perhaps this policy might change. I think it has to change.

On the hemispheric economic agenda, I commend the Administration's rhetorical support for the Free Trade Area of the Americas, but the critical question is whether it will serve the interests as identified by Mr. Menendez with regard to labor and the environment, and whether it will also respond to the legitimate agenda put forth by Brazil on agricultural subsidies, or intellectual property rights, or anti-dumping and subsidies.

On the social scene where poverty encompasses nearly one-third of the population, the President is to be commended for the Millennium Challenge Account, but as we have just heard, we still do not know if that account will even apply to the poor in Latin America.

Rather than continue to critique the policy, however, I would like to propose an alternative approach for all of you to consider. I believe that to achieve our objectives in the region today we need to listen more than lecture. Since September 11th and since the war in Iraq our policy has been focused, with good reason, on terrorism, but that is not a policy that fits all regions.

The question in Latin America is whether it is possible to achieve our ends by acting alone. Let me just pose four issues for you to think about.

First, on trade, the North American Free Trade Agreement has been a success for what it was designed to do. It reduced trade and investment barriers, and tripled trade and investment. But it has been a failure in what it omitted.

It did not answer the question of development, and the development gap between Mexico and its northern neighbors has widened. It did not address the issue of migration, and migration issue has worsened in many way. It did not talk about policy coordination, or indeed did not address the critical question of integration, which is more fundamental than the trade issue.

The countries of North America have accelerated their integration, but we have not created the institutions or procedures that could either head off crises or that could take advantage of great opportunities.

But it is a bit unusual to begin talking about North American trade in the hemisphere—I am focusing on North America, but I think there are three good reasons to do so.

First, there are no two nations in the world that have a greater effect on us than our two largest trading partners, and, specifically, in terms of our economy, immigration, and energy.

Secondly, if Mexico cannot find a path through the free trade agreement of NAFTA to the first world economy, then I dare say that the other nations of the Americas are not going to look toward the Free Trade Area of the Americas in solving their economic problems.

And conversely, if we can find a way to reduce the development gap between Mexico and its northern neighbors, this would be a shining model for the rest of the region.

I would encourage following Congressman Menendez's suggestion that you hold your second hearing on North America specifically, address the question of immigration, and think also of what this Committee and Congress could do on its own.

For 40 years, Congress has had an inter-parliamentary group meeting with Mexico and a separate one with Canada. If it brought Canada and Mexico under the same roof and create an inter-parliamentary group on North America, it could begin to address a series of issues that we at American University have tried to address with our new Center for North American Studies; issues such as a customs union, such as a North American passport among groups that travel frequently across the borders, such as a North American plan for transportation and infrastructure.

There are many different issues that have remained unaddressed because we continue to pursue our concerns in North American in a dual bilateral context rather than in a partnership of North America.

Secondly, the Inter-American Democratic Charter does represent a very significant step forward in trying to strengthen democracy in the hemisphere, but it is clearly inadequate. If it were not, we would not face the kind of crises that we face in Venezuela and in the Andes today.

So the question is where do we go from here for that charter. I have done an extensive analysis of it. I think the first problem is conceptual. There are literally s laundry lists of definitions of democracy, and therefore it is very hard to pinpoint what is essential about democracy from what is desirable, and what are the nature of the threats that are faced in Latin America and what is the best way to respond to them.

I think a definition should start with a precise one based on democracy as a system of government in which the people choose their leaders at regular intervals in a free environment, and their leaders have effective authority. The threats correspond to different levels of political development.

After sorting out definitions, however, the critical question is what to do about the threats, and there perhaps Congressman Delahunt's idea of a Center for Democracy, perhaps a nongovernmental center or an intergovernmental one similar to the Inter-American Commission on Human Rights could play a critical role if it could write hard-hitting reports each year on where democracy is failing or succeeding in each of the countries of the Americas, and submit those reports to the OAS for hard discussion about what should be done by the OAS, not just by the OAS secretary general who has played such a critical and positive role in Venezuela, but by the entire OAS.

Beyond that, we need to think about ways to multilateralize our approach to the nondemocracies in the hemisphere, to Cuba and to Haiti as well.

The third issue is poverty and exclusion, and here we know that education and growth can reduce income disparities, and a progressive and effective fiscal system is critical to ensuring that the gains that come to an entire nation as a result of free trade are distributed among both the winners as well as the losers. A free market is not sufficient for reducing that gap.

Indeed, in the first stage of free trade very often the gap is widened. For example in Mexico, the northern states of Mexico have grown 10 times faster than the central and southern states, widening the gap within Mexico.

You need compensatory mechanisms such as perhaps a social investment fund or a fund on education that could be funded by deferred spending that would have been used for, for example, purchasing supersonic aircraft, which is something that Chile recently has done, and other countries are considering as well.

Finally, on drugs and terrorism and the broader issue of security, there is a lot of room for us to narrow the gap between our conception of security in the post-9/11, and Latin America's concern about small arms trafficking, denuclearization, demining, and I hope in Mexico in the next week we will try to do that.

But more broadly, to succeed on the drug issue we need to understand that we need to deal with it on the health side, the demand side of the equation, and we need to do it in a much more collaborative way than we have managed up until now. And on terrorism, the same applies.

So just to conclude and allow you time for questions, I think we are at a crossroads. Latin America could continue down the road toward deepening its democracies and building a collective system in defense of democracy, toward completing the Free Trade Area of the Americas, and making it consistent with interests and values related to labor and the environment, or it could move backwards in time toward instability and toward dictatorship, toward widening disparities.

The United States also faces a crossroads, not just in this hemisphere, but beyond that in defining the nature of our leadership and the nature of the world in which we want to live. We could pursue our interests by ourselves, focusing exclusively on our fear stemming from 9/11. We could ignore the interests and the perspectives of our closest neighbors, or we could follow the vision first defined by Franklin Roosevelt and Harry Truman that said that multilateralism is not just a means when we may need it after failing in a particular part of the world, but it is also an end in itself, because the nature of our relationships with our neighbors requires that we find space for them to define their future, and we need to listen and adjust our own definition accordingly.

And in the long term this will do more to promote our values and our interests in the hemisphere, do more to reduce the development gap between the United States and Latin America, do more to create the kind of vision of the Americas that could serve as a model for the relationship between industrialized and developing countries.

Thank you, Mr. Chairman.

[The prepared statement of Mr. Pastor follows:]

PREPARED STATEMENT OF ROBERT A. PASTOR, VICE PRESIDENT OF INTERNATIONAL AFFAIRS, AMERICAN UNIVERSITY

Mr. Chairman, Mr. Menendez, Members of the Committee. It is a great honor to be invited to offer an assessment of the challenges facing the United States in the Americas, the policies of the George W. Bush Administration, and the opportunities that could be seized by an alternative approach. I commend this Committee for focusing on our closest neighbors at a time when the attention of the Administration and most of the country is elsewhere.

THE STATE OF THE AMERICAS

Many in Latin America had high expectations for U.S.-Latin American relations when George W. Bush was elected President. He alone of the two major candidates had given a speech devoted to the region, and he promised that if elected, the region would not be an "after-thought;" it would be central to his foreign policy. As a former Governor of the border state of Texas, Bush had also signaled to the new Mexican President Vicente Fox and the re-elected Prime Minister of Canada Jean Chretien that he would give the highest priority to the two closest neighbors of the United States. He has not delivered.

During the past two years, the United States has lost jobs and Latin America's economy has contracted. The Free Trade Area of the Americas (FTAA) is in grave danger as Brazil insists that agricultural subsidies and anti-dumping legislation should be on the agenda, and the United States rejects that. Secretary of State Colin Powell acknowledged during the swearing-in ceremony of Assistant Secretary of State Roger Noriega that Latin America was suffering from "a level of dissatisfaction with the quality of democracy and the results of economic reform."

"Dissatisfaction" is an under-statement. This past week, a progressive Bolivian President was tossed out of office by a mob. Bolivia's neighbors in the Andes—Peru, Ecuador, Colombia, and especially Venezuela—seem on the precipice of chaos or conflict. The economy of Brazil, the engine in South America, is stalled, and its neighbor, Argentina remains in default on its international debt. Relations with our two closest neighbors—Canada and Mexico—have sunk to their lowest level in decades, undermined by divergent perceptions of September 11th and the war in Iraq. Had there been the partnership in North America that had been promised, one could have imagined that the leaders of the three countries would have met on the White House lawn on September 12th to declare that the attack was aimed at all of North America and that they would respond as one. Alas, that did not occur.

The central issues in the hemisphere remain development, the consolidation of democracy, poverty, and security against terror, crime, and drug-trafficking. With the end of the Cold War and the spread of democracy and freer-trade regimes, the nations of the Americas finally found themselves using the same language and pursuing similar—if not the same goals. The new post-9/11 US focus on security combined with the pre-emptive war strategy enunciated by the Bush Administration has re-opened the gulf that had historically kept the U.S. and Latin America apart, and it has re-ignited suspicions of U.S. motives. Thus, your Committee's deliberation offers Congress and the Administration a chance to step-back and ask how we might reduce the division and advance our hemispheric interests and values.

THE RESPONSE BY THE BUSH ADMINISTRATION

I will leave it to Assistant Secretary Noriega to state the Administration's positions, and I will not use my scarce time to critique the policy as I would prefer to try to sketch out alternatives. But let me just briefly say that, in my view, the most striking feature of the Bush Administration's policy is that there is so little of it, and that the declared policies seem so inconsistent with the Administration's deeds.

Secretary Powell should be credited for signing the Inter-American Democratic Charter in Lima, but what does that act mean when others in the Administration support a coup d'etat in Venezuela, only to be chastised by the rest of the inter-American community? What does our declared support for democracy mean when U.S. Ambassadors take sides in a presidential election in Bolivia and El Salvador? Does this Administration not realize that Latin Americans remain suspicious of U.S. declarations on democracy because we sometimes undermined democratically-elected leaders, who were anti-American?

On the hemispheric economic agenda, when one of the most important economies in South America went bankrupt, then-US Treasury Secretary Paul O'Neill dismissed the country with a crude remark. Trade Representative Zoellick ought to be congratulated for his support for the Free Trade of the Americas, and President Bush for seeking a good relationship with the new Brazilian President Lula da Silva, but what does that mean when the United States ignores Brazil's trade agenda and tries to undermine it by pursuing separate deals?

On the social crisis where poverty threatens nearly one-third of the region's population, the President was courageous in proposing the Millenium Challenge Account, but it is still not clear if any of it will help the region's impoverished.

No American would question the necessity of a strategy against terror. The issue is whether an exclusive pursuit of that goal in the Americas is productive. The Administration has not made the case that there is the kind of threat in the Americas that would justify ignoring other US interests described above.

AN ALTERNATIVE APPROACH TO THE AMERICAS FOR THE 21ST CENTURY

A new approach to the Americas needs to begin with some humility and a willingness to bridge the post-Iraq gap. The United States needs to realize that its power has limits and obligations. U.S. power can compel other governments to take our agenda seriously, but if we brandish it or ignore other views, we unintentionally invite resistance or simply no cooperation.

To achieve our objectives in the region (and elsewhere), we need to listen more and lecture less. And while most of the rest of the Americas disagreed with our entry into Iraq, the governments need to find ways to respond to the U.S. agenda even as they pursue their own. An opportunity presents itself at the forthcoming Special Conference on Security of the OAS. Much of Latin America prefers a security agenda based on disarmament, curbs on small arms sales, denuclearization, demining (only the US and Cuba have not approved of the Ottawa Treaty) while the United States seeks its security agenda. Why not pursue all of these objectives?

Let me offer a brief agenda for the Americas of four opportunities—a North American Community, a stronger system for defending democracy, a new emphasis on poverty and exclusion, and an alternative approach to drugs and terrorism.

1. A North American Community. It may seem unusual to begin a discussion of new approaches to the hemisphere by focusing on North America, but there are several good reasons. First, no two nations affect the U.S. more, and no two nations are affected by the US more, than Canada and Mexico. Second, if Mexico cannot climb to the first world through NAFTA, and indeed, if the development gap between Mexico and its two richer neighbors continues to widen, then other nations in the Americas should legitimately ask whether free trade is the solution or the problem. Conversely, if Mexico succeeds, and if the United States demonstrates it can listen and adjust to the concerns of its neighbors, then the prospects for a collaborative hemisphere increase. .

At American University, I have established and direct a new Center for North American Studies with the purpose of educating a new generation to the complexities of the largest free-trade area in the world in terms of gross product and population. Social and economic integration among the three countries has accelerated since NAFTA, but the three governments have failed to respond to the problems—externalities—that accompany a wider market. Thus, we have had peso crises, divisions on immigration, trucking, sugar, and softwood lumber, and we virtually ignored the central issue of Mexico's development, and the gap has widened. We can never solve the problem of undocumented migration and never develop a true trilateral partnership unless and until the development gap separating Mexico and its two northern neighbors could be significantly reduced. A North American Development Fund, which could be managed by existing banks, could do this.

Let me request that you consider a second hearing specifically on North America and look beyond NAFTA to the issue of integration and policy coordination. There is much to be learned from the European experience—both in terms of what we should adapt and what we should avoid. Beyond that, Congress could take the lead in merging the two bilateral parliamentary commissions with Mexico and Canada to create a new Inter-Parliamentary Group on North America that could consider new initiatives, including a North American passport, a Customs Union, a Permanent Court on Trade and Investment to replace the ad hoc dispute settlement mechanism, and a North American Plan for Infrastructure and Transportation.

The successful pursuit and implementation of a *Free Trade Area of the Americas*, a goal that I support, is not likely unless we can demonstrate the power of the first example—with Mexico and North America. We should not postpone FTAA negotiations; we should move forward as rapidly as possible, but we need to be responsive to the region's agenda, and our own interests in labor and the environment.

2. Instilling Substance into the Democratic Charter. The Santiago Commitment of 1991 represented an historic step by the inter-American community toward building a collective defense for democracy. The Democratic Charter signed in Lima on September 11, 2001 represented another important step, but its inadequacy is demonstrated by the political turbulence in the Andes. What more is needed?

The first problem is conceptual. The Charter is a long list of definitions of democracy, which makes its defense actually more difficult. If the inter-American community had to respond to every threat, including economic setbacks, it would respond to none, which is largely the case. We need a precise definition, and here's one: a system of government whereby the people choose their leaders at regular intervals in a free environment, and the leaders have effective authority. The principal threats to democracy correspond to different levels of political development. At the most tenuous level, governments face threats over the fairness of the electoral process (vertical accountability). At the transitional level, governments face problems when one branch of government oversteps its constitutional prerogative—e.g., when the President closes Congress, or the military overthrows the President (horizontal accountability). Finally, democracies face social and economic threats because they erode the foundation of democracy or because people hold democracy, rather than the incumbent, responsible.

Second, after sorting out the definition, the OAS should charge either a non-governmental body or a quasi-governmental one, similar to the Inter-American Commission on Human Rights, to do hard-hitting annual reports on the state of democracy in each of the countries of the Americas.

Third, the countries of the Americas need to develop a common multilateral strategy for acting on these reports. If there was a military threat, the Inter-American Defense Board could be invited. If the problem is the lack of judicial independence, leaders from the Supreme Courts of the Americas could visit the country to develop strategies for strengthening the judicial system.

Fourth, the leaders of the Americas could try to find common ground to advance democracy in a legitimate manner in Cuba and Haiti, the two remaining non-democratic countries in the Americas. In the case of Cuba, that might require a change in the historical approach by the United States, as most governments in Latin America find it difficult to promote democracy there while the United States maintains an embargo. The question for the United States is which approach is more likely to succeed. After forty years of an embargo, it seems obvious that this is a blunt instrument that Castro uses to blame all Cuba's ills; it is not an effective strategy for democracy.

3. Poverty and Exclusion. At its base, the protest in Bolivia, Venezuela, and Ecuador is a symptom of a far deeper crisis—the exclusion and increasing impoverishment of a widening band of poor people, many of whom are indigenous peoples. The problem is both an objective and a subjective one. We know that a country that grows and invests in its education can narrow income gaps. Chile has demonstrated that during the past 15 years. Freer trade and a more open market has helped India and China, the world's two most populous nations, to reduce poverty in the past decades, but in Mexico, freer trade has led the northern part of Mexico to grow ten times as fast as the southern part. A progressive and effective fiscal system is critical to ensure that the gains of trade are shared among those who lose because of increasing competition.

So the problem has to be addressed at two levels. At the objective level, more funds need to be invested in education and free-market reforms, including reducing trade and investment barriers, but more attention needs to be given to lifting the more deprived regions. The proposal of Congressman Menendez for a "social investment fund" could be targeted on this problem. At the level of perception, much more education needs to be undertaken to explain that barriers to trade and investment as, as Arthur Miller once wrote of "walls," "an expensive investment in denial."

Still another approach, which could combine an interest in disarmament and education, would be to establish an Education Fund for Democracies that would receive revenues from deferred defense expenditures that would have been spent for advanced weaponry and would use those funds for Education.

4. Drugs and Terrorism. The Bush Administration and its predecessors have used the language of "war" to attack both drug traffickers and terrorists, but the truth is that the proper metaphor is mega-crime because armies and law enforcement authorities cannot stop both menaces. Drugs need to be addressed as a health problem, and terrorists, by understanding their local roots and identifying the best strategy to pull them up by their roots. Tragically, we are unlikely to solve either problem; the only question is whether we can manage them better, and the answer is: of course, but only if you deal with all the dimensions of each issue, and only if you forge a bond of cooperation with all friendly nations. We haven't done either yet; we must do both soon.

CONCLUSION

Even if we addressed all four issues effectively, we would not have a 21st century defined by the Americas. An additional step is needed. The United States has to take our neighbors seriously and in a manner different from the past. This is possible now because of democracy and new bonds of economic collaboration, but it also requires negotiating a new set of rules and institutions that can bring more balance, while not sacrificing effectiveness, to inter-American relations.

The twin challenges for the US in the 21st century are, first, how we will define our leadership, and secondly, what kind of world do we want? These two questions are intimately related. At the end of the Second World War, Franklin D. Roosevelt and Harry Truman had a vision of US leadership establishing universal institutions that would shape the world in ways compatible with US ideals and interests.

We have forgotten that vision. Today, those who believe that we alone can defend ourselves argue with those who seek support from other nations. But today's multilateralists see it as a means to pursue our security—not as an end. FDR and Truman understood that it was both a means and an end. We need to return to their vision.

What has that got to do with the Americas? Everything. From our independence, we have proceeded to defend our national security in terms of three levels: first America; second, the Americas; and third, the world. We are now a global power, and no one believes that hemispheric isolation is possible, but we are equally foolish if we fail to take into account the importance of our neighbors in global security.

And so we return to our home in the Americas. It is here that we need to define a new approach to each other and thus to the world. First, let's focus on North America and build the institutions and a path for Mexico to reach a first world economy. Let's aim to reduce poverty and transform the war on drugs and terrorism into a genuinely collective campaign. Most important, let's plant our democratic institutions deeper into the collective soil of the Americas. Let us take the phrase, "the community of democracies" and instill real substance into it.

Mr. BALLENGER. We thank you. That was a rather interesting statement. A couple of things that I would like to bring up because I live in the textile area of this United States, and my industry, my job seekers have been hurt more by what they claim is NAFTA, but you know and I know that NAFTA worked beautifully for about the first 4 years until the economies of the Far East collapsed, and all of a sudden then—somebody figured out this idea of trans-shipments.

And when you saw that strike on the west coast where all of the containers got hung up there, and you realized the numbers that were coming into this country. Although people did complain a little bit, nobody paid much of attention to the fact that they were unloading those containers and shipping them to Mexico, and changing a few labels and coming back as part of NAFTA. Maybe we did not have a law in place to prevent this, or we did not enforce whatever law was necessary. Free trade is wonderful, but fair trade is even better—that is kind of the wailing cry back home now for all of the people who lost their jobs—NAFTA did it.

Well, in my considered opinion, NAFTA did not do it. It was the lack of Federal Government involvement in enforcing whatever laws we had. And then the sad part about it, I don't know what you can do, you mentioned the fact that northern Mexico profited so substantially by NAFTA and southern Mexico got nothing out of it, and I do not understand if a country's government misspends the prosperity that is gained by that, I do not see what we can do for it as individuals.

I would just like to throw those two comments out and see what you shoot at them.

Mr. PASTOR. Sure. I think, first of all, you recall that Ross Perot was the one who talked about——

Mr. BALLENGER. "Great sucking sound."

Mr. PASTOR [continuing]. NAFTA's "great sucking sound," and you recall that in the 7 years that followed that prediction the United States expanded the number of jobs by 23 million.

Mr. BALLENGER. I agree.

Mr. PASTOR. Now, I would not attribute the 23 million all to NAFTA, but it is clear that NAFTA did not hurt us with regard to jobs, and indeed, most of the clear estimates of how many jobs were lost as a result of NAFTA are dwarfed by the numbers that are created by creating a very formible economic unit.

I mean, North America is the largest Free Trade Area in the world today, larger than the European Union in terms of gross product, territory, and population as well. Our economies have become integrated to a great extent, and I think it has benefitted our three countries.

I do not think that China and Japan, for example, which have manipulated their currencies for an extended period of time, have played by those same rules, and I think that there are ways to deal with that and ways to ignore it, which is what we have largely been doing. But I would not blame Mexico, and indeed, I think that Mexico, the United States and Canada have benefitted from increasing free trade.

Now, let me get to the second question. It is not corruption that has led to the northern part of Mexico growing faster than the center and the south. It is the free market at will and it is the absence of a concerted development strategy. There was an implicit development strategy in NAFTA, and that was to invest larger amount of money in Mexico, but do it close to the border area.

When I have asked the large corporations why they did that, why do you invest in the border area when the cost of labor is three times what it is in the center and the south, when the pollution is so bad, when the turnover rate is 100 percent each year because the current implicit development strategy serves as a magnet drawing workers up from the center and the south to the border where they then cross the border, their answer was very simple.

There is no infrastructure, there is no way for us to invest in the center and the south. We could do more to reduce this disparity by creating a North America Investment Fund that would fund the infrastructure between the border and the center and the south of the country. There is no question that the returns on the investment for the United States would be dramatic. There would be no kind of foreign aid that you could possibly come up with anywhere in the world that would have as an immediate effect on the United States economy as that. Ninety cents out of every dollar of imports going into Mexico are to pay for United States products.

So we would do a lot to both balance Mexico's development, we would do much more to deal with the migration problem. The migration problem will never be solved until the development gap between Mexico and its neighbors is reduced. That could be done with a North American Investment Fund.

Mr. BALLENGER. I agree with you, but sadly, you are in a position to advise somebody, maybe they should try that, and I guess neither the Republicans nor the Democrats have done the job that they could have done.

Mr. PASTOR. Yes. I think this is an issue that is going to require a lot more education, a lot more focus. That is why I set up the Center for North American Studies at American, and why I am eager to work with all of you to make these ideas real, but it will take time.

Mr. BALLENGER. A very creative thought.

Mr. Menendez.

Mr. MENENDEZ. Thank you, Mr. Chairman. Dr. Pastor, let me thank you for your testimony. Much of it, I think, is very thought-provoking. We look forward to talking to you in the days ahead about some of these items, and I just want to follow up on your last point where you just said we cannot solve the problem of migration and develop a true trilateral partnership unless and until the development gap separating Mexico and its two northern neighbors could be significantly reduced.

You talked about this North American development, but how do you envision the fund being funded? Is it from the three countries involved? How is it that you would see that actually be deployed?

Mr. PASTOR. Well, I have no question in my mind that this is a far-ranging proposal that I am going to put forward. But I think that it is no more implausible than the idea that Vicente Fox would be able to overthrow the Institutional Revolutionary Party (PRI) after 70 years.

The World Bank has estimated that Mexico needs $20 billion a year in infrastructure investment over a 10-year period to fill its infrastructure deficit and to increase its rate of growth to 6 percent, double the United States rate of growth, which would reduce the development gap by 20 percent in a decade and change the perception of Mexico.

Once Mexico starts growing faster than us, the immigration issue will begin to change.

Where would the money come from? I think it has to come mostly from the United States. Of the $20 billion, $10 billion should come from United States and Canada, United States contributing 90 percent and Canada 10 percent.

With that pledge of $10 billion infrastructure investment from the United States and Canada, we go to Mexico and say, look, our people are not prepared to give you their taxpayers' money if your people are not prepared to pay taxes. Mexico right now pays taxes at the rate of roughly 11 to 12 percent of its GDP.

We will say to them you have got to double that, which would yield $10 billion in your contribution to the fund. If we are going to put this fund forward, you have got to contribute half way. That $20 billion, however, would have a tremendous effect.

I looked closely at the European Union's experience in reducing the development gap between the richest and poorest countries, and there is a lot to learn from that experience both as to what to adopt and what to avoid. But that which worked best was investment in infrastructure and post-secondary education, rural community education.

So I have no doubt that this will not be easy, convincing your colleagues to put forth $9 billion a year for a Mexican development fund, but I am persuaded that——

Mr. MENENDEZ. You do not mean a year?

Mr. PASTOR. Ten billion dollars a year for 10 years from the United States and Canada.

Mr. MENENDEZ. Oh, $100 billion.

Mr. PASTOR. That is right, which is a little bit more than what we have just decided to do for Iraq for 1 year, and I think the return on the investment for the United States economy would exceed by a factor of a thousand what the investment in Iraq would do, and this is a long-term project, and this is only possible with a very dramatic change in our perspective about North America and our neighbors.

Mr. MENENDEZ. That is a dramatic vision when you just heard me spar with the Secretary and the USAID administrator about less than a billion dollars for the entire hemisphere to get, but I understand the nature of what you are suggesting. We might have to find other partners in that process, but I appreciate the vision.

And finally, you say about poverty and exclusion, and you refer to a country that grows and invests in its education can narrow income gaps, and you point to Chile that has done so during the last 15 years.

How do you envision exactly that taking place? None of the things that I see before us, the millennium challenge or anything else, incentivizes a country on its own to make that investment in its people. How is it that you would envision that taking place?

Mr. PASTOR. Well, it has got to be aid that is much more steeply conditioned than we have seen in the past, and it has to be one that focuses much more precisely on the nature of the educational challenge in each country.

Many of the countries spend a good deal of money on education, but they either spend it at the university system by subsidizing what are relatively speaking wealthier individuals than they do at the primary and secondary levels. Other countries need to contemplate rural community colleges that would lift the economies.

That is what I found in Spain and Portugal, which was the most impressive to me. They invested in community colleges in small, rural areas, and what happened is that they brought the university-educated, trained teachers back to these community colleges from the capital, and big cities, and that in effect lifted the primary and secondary education because they put their kids in those schools, and it had a transforming effect in the rural areas that Mexico has not had the chance and no other country with the exception of Chile and Costa Rica, for example, have really done in Latin America.

Mr. MENENDEZ. Thank you for your observations and for coming today and testifying.

Mr. PASTOR. Yes, sir.

Mr. BALLENGER. Congressman Weller.

Mr. WELLER. Thank you, Mr. Chairman. Mr. Pastor, good to see you again. I recall when I was an observer for the Palestinian elections with you and President Carter back in 1996. Unfortunately, things have not turn out as quite has we had hoped they would do at that time. Those were very hopeful times for all of us.

I just want to comment on some of your statements, but I have one question in particular. Mr. Delahunt and I share the desire for creating some sort of institution that will foster democracy in the Western Hemisphere, and in my view, fostering the concept of the true meaning of public service for all elected officials, and those who have the opportunity to serve in the democracies in the Western Hemisphere in positions of government.

I noted in your comments you think that the Administration perhaps lectures more than—and not listens enough, and at the same time your thoughts about the Center for Democracy suggests that the Center for Democracy should grade, judge and essentially lecture. So you might, you know, something to think about.

Again, I believe that the Center for Democracy should, or whatever we would call it, is an idea that deserves bipartisan support—Mr. Delahunt and I have discussed this—to really foster the true concept of public service by those of us who are elected.

Also I note you made some comments regarding interference perhaps in elections in certain Latin American countries, usually in regard to comments made regarding former communist guerilla leaders who are now candidates for office. I think in the news reports that I have seen, and certainly notice that some of my congressional colleagues never hesitated to interject themselves working in concert with groups which perhaps impact an election in certain countries of Latin America either.

But the question that I would really like to direct to you, and the question that I had for Secretary Noriega is one that has been a frustration of mine.

You know, Colombia is a very important country, and as I noted earlier it is one of the most longstanding democracies in not only Latin America but in the Western Hemisphere, and an important nation with great history. And they have been fighting, you know, narco-funded guerrillas, both left and right, for some time, over the last generation.

And like my colleagues, I meet with a lot of human rights groups coming through, and one thing I have always noticed, and I ask this of you because I think you are more center left and I am more center right with our perspective on things, but you know, human rights groups always seem to do a pretty good job of, you know, highlighting the atrocities of right-wing groups.

But when we have seen what has occurred in Colombia, particularly with the FARC and the left-wing groups out there that is murdering, slaughtering electing officials, kidnapping presidential candidates, and of course, committing terrible crimes throughout Colombia, intimidating the electorial process, we hear little.

And I was just wondering from your perspective with all of the work you have done in Latin America, the work you have done through the Carter Center, why is that? Why does the left tend to focus on the atrocities committed by the right, and then you see little attention or effort to draw attention to the atrocities committed by left-wing groups?

Mr. PASTOR. Well, you will have to ask those groups because that is not what I happen to believe, but I could just say as an analyst I think that may be because they hold the governments to a higher degree of responsibility than they do to guerilla groups.

But leaving that aside, I think that——

Mr. WELLER. Yes, but these—I am talking about the parliamentarians in Colombia. I am not talking about the freely-elected government of Colombia, or President Uribe or President Pastrana. What I am talking about is the paramilitaries are designated the right-wing group there. Then you have got the two left wing, and they all are funded through narco-trafficking, we all know that, and they are all committing horrible atrocities.

The point is that when human rights groups come into my office they never talk about the left wingers, and I am just curious from your perspective why is that?

Mr. PASTOR. Well, Mr. Chair, or it may be premature as he is walking out, I think you are absolutely right that all three groups, both the paramilitaries, and the FARC and the ELN and the drug traffickers have engaged in gross and systematic violations of human rights, and they ought to all be condemned for that.

I think there were certain human rights groups that were concerned that the paramilitary groups were being supported either passively or directly by the military, which may have been one of the reasons.

But leaving aside the nature of the criticism, I think the challenge in Colombia, and I think President Uribe has done an enormous amount in a short time, and that is demonstrated by the popularity that he has from his people right now, is to make it clear to all of those—to both the guerilla groups and to the paramilitaries that he is not willing to concede territory or to concede the war to them, but that he is willing to negotiate with them an exit from the war should they take it.

There are some examples that were pointed to earlier that suggests that some are taking it, but a great many are not taking it, and that is why I think support is necessary from the United States. It would be even better if it were greater support from some of his neighbors in the area.

But to bring it back to your question, one of the reasons that human rights groups were concerned about the paramilitaries was because of suspicion that perhaps some military had been working with them.

Mr. WELLER. [Presiding.] Thank you. I know that we are down to the last question here, Mr. Delahunt, and then we will be ready to conclude our hearing. Chairman Ballenger has departed, and I guess I am the Chair, so my pleasure to yield——

Mr. DELAHUNT. Thank you.

Mr. WELLER [continuing]. To my colleague from Massachusetts.

Mr. DELAHUNT. Thank you for coming. You know, in response to the question by Mr. Weller, I think my own observations over the course of maybe the past 5 or 10 years, all of the groups in Colombia are significantly less ideological than they are just simply criminal syndicates at this point in time. I include what many will describe as right-wing to left-wing. I think the differences in terms of the groups is so murky now that it really just does not make any difference in terms of how they are described. They all seem to be equally acknowledged as systematically undermining democracy and violating human rights, and at the same time obviously committing atrocities.

You were talking about in terms of assistance and conditionality. I think the distinction, and I agree with Mr. Menendez in terms of when we speak of environmental and labor standards, to get the attention of those governments to initiate reform, I would submit, I would be interested in your observation, that it has to be part of trade agreements—whether it be FTAA or whether it be a bilateral trade agreement. That is where the leverage is in terms of insistence on the kind of judicial reform, regulatory reform, strengthening of democratic institutions.

And I came to Congress with that belief, and the more I observe Latin America the more convinced I become of the correctness of that particular opinion.

You know, the Washington consensus, you have heard the testimony here, we have had 10 years where some governments, and again in fits and starts, have made efforts to institute economic reform, but the reality is the political support has eroded simply because these societies have not seen the benefit, and given the fact that the United States, our image in the hemisphere to a great degree has eroded because of differences on Iraq, but as well as the lack of what they see as no change in their living standards added to that.

And again, that is just an observation as far as the conditionality being more effective in terms of, again, FTAA negotiations or bilateral trade agreements. Respond.

Mr. PASTOR. Well, first, let me also agree with your point on Colombia, to return to Congressman Weller's point, in 1998, I was asked by both the FARC and the Colombian government to try to negotiate the release of 77 soldiers from the FARC, and I went there and I negotiated with them. And it was clear to me then that they had lost their ideology a long time ago, and that they were the best fed, the best clad rebels I had ever seen anywhere because of their associations with the drug traffickers, and that remains to this day.

With regard to your principal question, it is quite appropriate for the United States in its trade negotiations to insist on adherence to global labor and environmental standards, and to look toward ways in which those standards can be enforced just as the other provisions of any trade agreement have enforcement mechanisms as well.

I know there are some countries that are not in favor of that, but by and large, if they have already signed these agreements at the International Labor Organization or they have signed at Kyoto, which most of them have done anyway, then in theory they have already accepted the standards, and so it should not be an imposition on the part of the United States to say this is part of the agreement. I think it is quite appropriate.

The hard part in all of these countries, as you correctly pointed out, is to try to find a way to show the people that these agreements are working to their advantage, because I think you are quite correct that there is widespread feeling throughout Latin America that they have not, that what has been called neo-liberalism has not benefitted them.

Part of that perception is right and part is wrong. As consumers, they have benefitted enormously from cheaper products that are higher quality as a result of increasing competition in trade.

Mr. DELAHUNT. But the perception really has carried the day, if you will, as Mr. Menendez said earlier. My sense is that the perception, which is their reality, has actually reenforced the disparity.

To pose a question to anybody from the Administration and elsewhere, let us speak to Mexico, let us talk about median income, as to disparity. Is there empirical data that establishes that there has been a change in terms of median household income? Where are the real tangible benefits that I think would—you know, and they run parallel—support the nurturing and growth of democratic institutions as opposed to elections?

We have elections all over Latin America, but——

Mr. PASTOR. Yes, I have started, obviously, and focused on Mexico and North America because I think this is really quite key. If we cannot succeed there, then talking about extending beyond it is not going to work.

If you look closely at the effect of NAFTA on Mexico, you will see something very interesting. You look beyond the question of whether wages overall or on average have increased or declined, and you disaggregate, you find that those parts of Mexico that have been plugged into NAFTA and plugged into trade with the United States, they have really zoomed ahead. They have benefitted enormously. And those parts of Mexico that have no connection, that are not really into the trading system, that they have fallen down very far.

So you average them out and you see no change. But you disaggregate and you realize part of the problem is that the trade has not been extended to the poor areas, and the reason it has not been extended is because we have relied solely on the market, and that is where you do need the investments in infrastructure, the investments in education in the poor areas.

We could wait for 100 years, as the United States did after the Civil War, for the South to rise again, and the market to correct itself, but I think we are living in a different world today. We do not want to wait for 100 years.

Mr. DELAHUNT. I would suggest it is very dangerous to do that.

Mr. PASTOR. It is very dangerous.

Mr. DELAHUNT. And again, your figures of 10 years and $10 billion is rather dramatic, but I do not know if you were here when I encouraged Secretary Noriega to think large. I mean, we have already spent 79 plus 87 billion in Iraq, or we will have shortly. To be candid, I mean, that is only a down payment. But again to incentivize governments, whether it be Mexico or—well, take Mexico off the table for a minute and talk the rest of Latin America, you incentivize them to create that social investment in areas that are not impacted by trade, which is basically manufacturing jobs I think is the right direction. That is why we have been working on this Center for Democracy and marrying it with the concept of Mr. Menendez's social investment fund, and we are talking of all Latin America, so those figures are right.

And also, just for your information, I have an amendment that is in State Department authorization, which I will be happy to give to you, it is a report on democracy in the Western Hemisphere. One finding I will read:

> "Although 34 out of 35 countries in the Western Hemisphere have held elections for civil leaders of national, regional and local governments, many of these countries have failed to successfully develop independent democratic institutions, transparent and accountable government, and effective means of guaranteeing the rule of law which are key components of a fully functioning democracy,"

and it requires the Secretary of State some 90 days after enactment of the reauthorization of DOS to make a report outlining the assessment of health of democracy in the hemisphere. I think that is the place to start.

Mr. PASTOR. If I may use that to respond to your earlier comment as well, Congressman. I think we should listen more and lecture less, but the idea that I had for this democracy institute or whatever you want to call it was that it would be genuinely multinational just like the Inter-American Commission on Human Rights.

The United States can play a leading role perhaps with the center here just as we did on human rights policy in the 1970s with our human rights reports, but for long-term effectiveness what really made a big difference for Latin America's human rights was the Inter-American Commission on Human Rights, and the Inter-

American Court on Human Rights, which spoke very forthrightly to all of Latin America, and really did have an enormous impact.

So this is a very good idea. It is not a question of us lecturing, it is question of distinguished individuals from all over the region speaking honestly as to what needs to be done and what should be done.

Mr. DELAHUNT. An Inter-American Faculty.

Mr. WELLER. If the gentleman would yield.

Mr. Pastor, should Mr. Delahunt or others have additional questions they would like to submit to you, I am sure you would be happy to respond to them in writing for the record?

Mr. PASTOR. I would.

Mr. WELLER. Okay. Well, thank you, and I appreciate the private sector panel, Mr. Pastor, for appearing before our Subcommittee today, and thank the Members for participating as well. It has been a useful hearing. Thank you.

This Subcommittee hearing is adjourned.

[Whereupon, at 4:36 p.m., the Subcommittee was adjourned.]

APPENDIX

Material Submitted for the Hearing Record

Responses from the Honorable Roger F. Noriega, Assistant Secretary of State for Western Hemisphere Affairs, U.S. Department of State, to questions submitted for the record by the Honorable Cass Ballenger, a Representative in Congress from the State of North Carolina, and Chairman, Subcommittee on the Western Hemisphere

Mr. Ballenger's Question:

As you know, Bolivia is in turmoil after weeks of violence and the resignation of their democratically elected president. Although the Vice President has taken over and the violence has subsided, the political tension remains. The issues that led to the unrest seem not to have been solved. Even the new President has indicated that the crisis is not yet over in Bolivia. What can we expect to happen in the next few weeks, years?

Mr. Noriega's Response:

President Mesa currently enjoys an 80 percent popular approval rating in Bolivia, but he lacks a political base and faces significant pressure from radical opposition groups. Mesa must make several difficult choices in the next few weeks and months that may lead to renewed protests by the opposition. Mesa has said he will revise the hydrocarbons law in January to boost the Bolivian Government's share of oil and gas revenues and hold a referendum on the export of natural gas in March. Mesa has also publicly pledged to continue the government's counternarcotics programs, including eradication in the Chapare.

The U.S. has supported the democratic and constitutional government of President Mesa, reprogramming approximately $12 million in already allocated DA, ESF, and ACI funds to fast-disbursing, labor intensive projects in the politically tense city of El Alto and provided under the continuing resolution $8 million in FY 2004 ESF funds to help the Bolivian Government close its 2003 budget gap. We are organizing a Bolivia Support Group meeting, tentatively scheduled for January 16 in Washington, to increase economic and diplomatic support from the international community. With this support, we hope the Mesa Government will be able to withstand pressure from radical opposition over the next year.

Mr. Ballenger's Question:

President Lula da Silva of Brazil and President Kirchner of Argentina seem to have some influence in Bolivia, possibly even with Evo Morales and his party. Has the State Department discussed working with the governments of Brazil and Argentina to help the democratic government of Bolivia?

Mr. Noriega's Response:

The Departments of State and Treasury are organizing with Mexico a Bolivia Support Group meeting tentatively scheduled for January 16. The group will consist of European and Latin countries, including Brazil and Argentina, and will seek to boost international economic and political support for Bolivia. In addition to our multilateral efforts, we have reached out to the Brazilian and Argentine governments individually, encouraging both to be supportive of President Mesa and Bolivian democracy.

Mr. Ballenger's Question:

The WTO decision on bananas is one of several sources of resentment towards the United States in the Caribbean. What initiatives can be undertaken to reach out to the nations of the Caribbean to make our relations more constructive?

Mr. Noriega's Response:

We enjoy close and constructive relations with the Caribbean based on shared history, values, culture, tradition, and objectives. The President met with four Caribbean leaders in New York in September, and Secretary of State Powell had a very productive meeting with a number of Caribbean Foreign Ministers in Santiago, Chile, last June, and more recently in Washington last November.

The Third Border Initiative (TBI), announced by President Bush in Quebec in 2001, is an opportunity for the U.S. to deepen its cooperation with its Caribbean neighbors on issues of mutual interest and ensure the prosperity and security of our neighborhood. Under the TBI umbrella, the United States is engaging the nations of the Caribbean to work together to achieve our shared goals of a stable, secure and economically prosperous region.

I met with all Caribbean Ambassadors in October to discuss in detail our plans to broaden our mutual cooperation under the Third Border Initiative. The goal of the TBI is to strengthen the capabilities of Caribbean countries and institutions to address security, economic, political and social problems and prevent their spillover to the United States. As part of Congress' ESF appropriation, we provided $3 million for the Third Border Initiative for the 2003 Fiscal Year. Our funding request for the 2004 Fiscal Year was $9 million. We understand that the Omnibus Spending Bill earmarks $4 million for TBI; we would direct these funds primarily at homeland security related activities. We hope the Third Border Initiative will improve an already strong partnership with the democratic nations of CARICOM and the Dominican Republic.

Beyond this, we and our partners among the democratic nations of the Caribbean have been working closely together on a broad variety of fronts. Among these are the fight against narcotics trafficking, terrorism and terrorist financing, the oversight of offshore financial sectors, and our joint commitment to fight the HIV/AIDS pandemic that has so severely affected the peoples of the Caribbean.

Mr. Ballenger's Question:

A recent trip to Colombia, and an earlier trip to the Tri-Border region have indicated that communities with possible connections to ME terrorists are raising money through the sale of pirated goods, arms dealing and drug trafficking.

What are we doing to address this issue? Are we pursuing a comprehensive strategy, in conjunction with host countries, to track and interdict these activities?

Mr. Noriega's Response:

The Tri-border area has long been a focal point for radical Islamic fundraising in Latin America, although such activity is not confined to the Tri-border region. The dominant group is Lebanese Hizballah. Hamas is also present to a lesser degree. While there is a large Lebanese, Syrian, and Palestinian expatriate population in the region, the vast majority of Arab-origin communities has no terrorist financing ties. Arab-origin individuals residing in these areas have been productive in local communities for generations.

In response, the Department of State has helped establish a multilateral counterterrorism (CT) mechanism with the Tri-Border Area (TBA) countries: Argentina, Brazil, and Paraguay. These three countries formally invited the United States to participate in a mechanism built on the framework of the pre-existing "Tripartite Commission of the Triple Frontier," creating the "3+1" format. The "3+1" strategy is to focus on practical, preventive steps to combat terrorism by enhancing cooperation among Brazil, Argentina, Paraguay, and the United States to curb terrorist financing, strengthen borders, enhance law enforcement capabilities, improve intelligence sharing, and implement anti-terrorism legislation. Since 2002, the "3 + 1" group has met three times, and the US is in the process of providing over $1 million for CT finance training and technical assistance to the area.

We are also very concerned about the sale of pirated goods, arms dealing and drug trafficking in this region, and are working with the governments of Argentina, Brazil and Paraguay to combat these problems.

Mr. Ballenger's Question:

The U.S. has now detained three major suspected drug traffickers [from] Haiti. Has this had any impact on Haitian officials or others with ties to narcotics traffickers?

Mr. Noriega's Response:

The expulsions of three major suspected drug traffickers by the Haitian government from Haiti to the U.S. represent major successes for counter-narcotics efforts in Haiti. We would like to see more cooperation between Haitian and U.S. law enforcement authorities.

The Department of Justice is responsible for questioning trafficking suspects and assessing and acting on resulting information. It is still too early to tell how these expulsions will affect those in Haiti with ties to narcotics traffickers. However, where we have credible information of ties to drug trafficking, by officials or others, we will not hesitate to take appropriate action. The magnitude of Haiti's trafficking problem clearly requires sustained efforts to overcome.

Mr. Ballenger's Question:

The new OAS envoy to Haiti, Ambassador Terence Todman, has identified the need to establish a secure environment in Haiti in order to hold new elections. Is the Administration prepared to provide significant resources to expand the OAS police monitoring mission?

Mr. Noriega's Response:

U.S. Government has provided $2.1 million of the $6.2 million provided to date to the OAS Special Mission, including $650,000 for the international police monitoring mission.

We plan to continue to provide support, within available resources, to the OAS Special Mission in Haiti, particularly its security component. Our goal remains improved public security that will allow formation of a credible, neutral, and independent electoral council, leading to new legislative and local elections.

Before it holds new elections, Haiti clearly needs a more secure environment, in which politicians, journalists, and other members of civil society can freely exercise their constitutional rights to freedom of expression, assembly, and association. We have, in line with OAS Resolution 822 and in cooperation with our OAS partners, consistently urged the Government of Haiti to meet its responsibilities and take concrete measures to improve the climate of security. The government has to date failed to take minimal needed steps.

Mr. Ballenger's Question:

How can we better use U.S. foreign assistance to get at the root causes of poverty and corruption in the Hemisphere?

Mr. Noriega's Response:

Understanding that Assistant Administrator Franco has provided the Committee with a separate answer, I would like to briefly discuss the policy aspects of your question.

In our view, the surest way to alleviate poverty is economic growth through trade and sound fiscal policy combined with institutional reform. We therefore remain committed to the vision of the expansion of free trade throughout the hemisphere, but also recognizing that reforms of tax laws and pension, regulatory, and judicial systems are also needed in so many countries. Free trade agreements are about much more than tariffs—they are also about locking in favorable investment climates, encouraging good governance, enforcing environmental protection and workers rights, breaking the power of inefficient economic elites, and better preparing the nations of the hemisphere for an inevitably globalized world. This is what we are in the process of trying to encourage throughout the Western Hemisphere.

At the same time, we recognize the need to invest in the people of the region. In keeping with the Monterrey Consensus and the principles of the Millennium Challenge Account, we increasingly are targeting our assistance at those countries that need it the most and that have also demonstrated a capacity to use that assistance wisely with the best interest of their citizens at heart. We also hope to encourage those countries that at first don't quite "make the grade" for MCA assistance to redouble their efforts to become eligible.

There is no doubt that corruption remains a serious problem in the Hemisphere and is probably the single most important reason that the reforms of the past 20 years have not been as successful as we all would have liked. Part of the answer lies in collective action against corruption and full implementation of the terms of the Inter-American Convention Against Corruption. We are also expanding our bilateral anti-corruption efforts. For example, we are working on developing a new $3 million anti-corruption project in Nicaragua to support the already considerable efforts of the Bolanos administration.

RESPONSES FROM THE HONORABLE ADOLFO A. FRANCO, ASSISTANT ADMINISTRATOR FOR LATIN AMERICA AND THE CARIBBEAN, U.S. AGENCY FOR INTERNATIONAL DEVELOPMENT, TO QUESTIONS SUBMITTED FOR THE RECORD BY THE HONORABLE CASS BALLENGER, A REPRESENTATIVE IN CONGRESS FROM THE STATE OF NORTH CAROLINA, AND CHAIRMAN, SUBCOMMITTEE ON THE WESTERN HEMISPHERE

LAC—CONCERNS OF BOLIVIA'S INDIGENOUS POPULATION

Mr. Ballenger's Question:

What is USAID's assessment of the key concerns of Bolivia's indigenous population? What is the Bolivian Government doing to address these concerns?

Mr. Franco's Response:

Bolivia remains a strategic ally of the U.S. in Andean counter-drug efforts and plays a leading role in South American initiatives for democratic reform and trade liberalization. Bolivia's indigenous population feels a deep sense of exclusion from the country's economic and social development. These feelings were clearly manifested during the new cycle of conflict that developed in September 2003, and culminated in the forced resignation of the constitutionally elected president. This conflict was due in large part to the concerns of the indigenous as well as poor Bolivians, that very little or no benefits would accrue to them from the sale of Bolivia's underground gas deposits to foreign buyers.

Since his appointment in November 2003, President Mesa has attempted to demonstrate his administration's commitment to working with the country's indigenous peoples. Recent actions include:

The creation of a Ministry of Indigenous Affairs, which is headed by an indigenous leader and includes two indigenous vice-ministers, one for the highlands and one for the lowlands. He has also named an indigenous leader as Minister of Education.

The creation of a Directorate of all major indigenous organizations in the country to organize the upcoming National Dialogue. The Dialogue is a forum for civil society to review Bolivia's Poverty Reduction Strategy and decide on the use of Highly Indebted Poor Countries (HIPC) debt forgiveness funds.

Meetings between President Mesa and indigenous groups to discuss key development priorities.

USAID's past efforts to assist the GOB expand its outreach to Bolivia's indigenous majority are continuing and several new initiatives have begun in the areas of political outreach, empowerment and economic growth. Examples include:

Support for the full implementation of the GOB's Judicial Reform package. This takes into account the 1999 Code of Criminal Procedures (CCP),that calls for respecting the customs and customary laws of Bolivia's indigenous people.

USAID's support for an OAS conflict prevention and resolution activity that will provide conflict resolution skills to GOB officials, civil society organizations, and indigenous groups.

In support of independent indigenous leaders, USAID has agreed to print and distribute 10,000 copies of the "Programa Tierra y Libertad" (PTL). The PTL was written by Walter Reynaga, a respected and independent indigenous leader. The reproduction will enable Mr. Reynaga and supporters of the PTL to stimulate debate on critical issues for Bolivia's development and broaden the PTL's base of support.

USAID is supporting efforts to reform traditional political parties by broadening and diversifying their membership. This will create a platform which reflects the concerns and interests of indigenous Bolivians.

USAID is helping to expand economic opportunities for indigenous communities engaged in the production and marketing of handicraft-based products, including jewelry, pottery, clothing, leather and wood. USAID-supported technical assistance and skills training in new designs, production techniques, and marketing, is expected to lead to global market access by indigenously owned and operated businesses.

USAID is contributing $5.0 million to the GOB's Emergency Employment Generation Program (PLANE), which provides temporary jobs in urban and rural areas. Most of the beneficiaries are the unemployed indigenous. To date, 372,000 jobs per month have been generated and approximately 4,500 projects implemented.

USAID contributed $745,000 of agricultural equipment and seed materials to assist the GOB's efforts to provide improved services to indigenous groups in the altiplano.

To assist the indigenous to secure titles to their lands, USAID has, in the last 10 years, invested more than $7.5 million in land titling activities. As a result, more than 1.6 million hectares of land now have secure titles.

USAID is collaborating with the GOB and European Union on a major land titling effort in the Chapare. An estimated 30,000 titles covering about 565,000 hectares will be issued by 2005. This project will strengthen the rule of law, democratic institutions, and citizen rights, including indigenous rights.

To assist the most food-insecure indigenous population in the altiplano, USAID's food security programs continue to reduce malnutrition, improve health care services, and incomes of 300,000 households located in 50 municipalities and 2,000 communities.

COFFEE INDUSTRY—USAID SUPPORT

Mr. Ballenger's Question:

USAID has made every effort to relieve the suffering and despair in Latin America. Through your economic development programs, you have helped thousands of people out of poverty. What specific programs are you undertaking to address the poverty caused by the decline of the coffee industry in Latin America? Are these programs working?

Mr. Franco's Response:

Since the advent of the coffee crisis in Central America in 2001, USAID, through both bilateral and regional programs, has provided emergency food aid and longer-term development assistance to thousands of displaced workers and small farmers. Development activities consist of helping farmers to produce a quality coffee bean for a premium price.

Small and medium-sized farmers and agricultural workers, who cannot produce a premium quality bean, are encouraged to diversify into other promising income generating areas. Activities include producing demand-driven products such as certified timber, various "green" products, new high-value horticultural crops, and involvement with tourism.

In 2002, USAID began to help producers improve their coffee bean quality under the Programa Regional de Café de Calidad (QCP), and to target the lucrative coffee niche markets worldwide, as we have successfully done in Haiti and more recently in Peru.

With USAID support, QCP is assisting premium quality bean producers to qualify for social and environmentally sound production certification on a regional scale. In 2004, it is expected that Central America will export 3,000 metric tons of certified coffee at premium plus prices.

Other examples of the program's success include the purchase of the entire 2002 premium coffee bean harvest of a large Guatemalan coffee association by a specialty U.S. Coffee Roaster, and the establishment of market linkages for the specialty coffee between 600 Salvadoran small farmers and Japan.

To promote income diversification, USAID is working with the non-traditional export association of Guatemala to support the expansion of information and communications technologies to take advantage of the Central America Free Trade Agreement (CAFTA), and other Free Trade Areas (FTAs).

The Association's Business Services Unit provides demand-driven assistance to small and medium farmers and rural enterprises to improve their competitiveness and tap new markets in areas such as eco-tourism, aquaculture, arts and crafts, and services. This unit has already generated 28 business alliances with a 1.7 to 1 match in resources from the local private sector.

Also, the Association has created a network of over 50 Electronic Business Development Centers with internet connections in rural areas to support investment and trade opportunities as well as governmental decentralization.

LAC—ROOT CAUSES OF POVERTY AND CORRUPTION IN THE HEMISPHERE

Mr. Ballenger's Question:

How can we better use U.S. foreign assistance to get at the root causes of poverty and corruption in the Hemisphere?

Mr. Franco's Response:

Widespread corruption, incomplete economic reforms, poor governance, the lack of rule of law, and inefficient and poorly functioning justice systems deprive countries of scarce revenues and discourage private investment flows for essential infrastructure, education, and skills development, and the opportunity to meaningfully participate in trade globalization.

Emerging economies must adopt and implement prudent, investment-friendly, pro-poor economic policies, and embrace freer trade to take advantage of their comparative and competitive advantages.

Also, more inclusive economic and social policies, property rights, rule-of-law, transparency, and anti-corruption must become central to better governance.

Combating poverty requires the commitment of national governments. Mexico has made sweeping political and economic progress. Brazil, Chile, Peru, and Costa Rica, have undertaken substantial reforms and are reaping the economic benefits.

As a model for the rest of the Hemisphere, the Chilean Government's limited role in the economy, openness to international trade and investment, and high domestic savings and investment rate all contributed to its high growth and a reduction by 50% of its poverty rate during the last decade

To mitigate poverty, USAID's priority programs will continue to focus on:

— Strengthening democracy and rule of law, combating corruption, and promoting policies that are conducive to stable, growing and inclusive economies.

— Supporting trade-led economic growth, and Trade Capacity Building (TCB) assistance for the priority TCB needs that the LAC countries have identified in order to transition to and benefit from free trade. We expect these efforts to culminate in a free trade area of the Americas agreement (FTAA) by 2005, the Central America Free Trade Agreement (CAFTA), and bilateral Free Trade Agreements (FTAs) with other cooperating countries, such as the Dominican Republic, Panama, and the Andean countries (initially, Colombia and Peru).

— Integrated approaches to poverty reduction. We are providing support to: reinforce citizen participation and a strong civil society for improving local governance; increase access by small and medium-sized businesses to micro-finance services, improve agriculturally-based household incomes, increase rural competitiveness, and expand education and job skills opportunities.

○

APEX
TP
9780160712098
76901945 – 79